MAJESTIC
IN HIS WRATH

MAJESTIC
IN HIS WRATH

A Pictorial Life of
Frederick Douglass

Frederick S. Voss
Introduction by Robert K. Sutton
Foreword by Waldo E. Martin, Jr.

Published for the National Portrait Gallery
and the National Park Service,
United States Department of the Interior,
by Smithsonian Institution Press
Washington and London

An exhibition at the National Portrait Gallery
February 10 through November 19, 1995.

This exhibition has been jointly organized by the
National Portrait Gallery, Smithsonian Institution,
and National Capital Parks-East, National Park
Service, United States Department of the Interior.
Partial support has been provided by the Frederick
Douglass Memorial and Historical Association, the
Frederick Douglass Housing Corporation, and the
Smithsonian Institution Special Exhibition Fund.

This book is dedicated to the memory of Professor
Sidney Kaplan, who suggested the Frederick
Douglass exhibition to the National Portrait
Gallery.

Library of Congress Cataloging-in-Publication Data
Voss, Frederick.
    Majestic in his wrath : a pictorial life of Freder-
ick Douglass / Frederick S. Voss; with an introduction by Robert K. Sutton; foreword by Waldo
E. Martin.
    Includes bibliographical references and index.
    ISBN 1-56098-522-4
    1. Douglass, Frederick, 1817?–1895—Pictorial
works.   2. Abolitionists—United States—Pictorial works.   3. Fugitive slaves—United States—
Pictorial works.   4. Afro-Americans—Pictorial
works.   I. Title.
E449.D75V67   1995
973.7′092—dc20
[B]   94-23940

British Library Cataloging-in-Publication data
available

00 99 98 97 96 95 5 4 3 2 1

♾ The paper used in this publication meets the
minimum requirements of the American National Standard for Permanence of Paper for
Printed Library Materials Z39.48–1984.

Cover illustration: Daguerreotype of Frederick
Douglass by an unidentified photographer, 8 ×
6.9 cm (3¹/₈ × 2³/₄ in.), circa 1850 after 1847 daguerreotype. National Portrait Gallery, Smithsonian Institution, Washington, D.C.

Frontispiece: Portrait of Frederick Douglass in
his sixties by Mathew Brady Studio (active 1844–
1883). Cabinet card, 30.5 × 27.9 cm (12 × 11 in.)
framed, circa 1880. Ronald L. Harris

Epigraph: Frederick Douglass by an unidentified
photographer. Ambrotype, 10.6 × 8.6 cm
(4³/₁₆ × 3³/₈ in.), 1856. National Portrait Gallery,
Smithsonian Institution, Washington, D.C.;
gift of an anonymous donor.

Photography Credits:
Eric Long: p. 98

Rolland White: cover, pp. ii, v, vii, x, xvi, xviii, 2,
10, 11, 18, 24, 25, 26, 29, 30, 32, 34, 36, 40, 50–51,
55, 64, 68–69, 70, 71, 72, 73, 78, 79, 82, 84, 87, 90,
91, 92, 93, 94–95, 99, 104
Oscar B. Willis: p. 96

For permission to reproduce any of the illustrations, correspond directly with the sources. The
Smithsonian Institution Press does not retain re-
production rights for these illustrations individu-
ally or maintain a file of addresses for photo
sources.

Printed in Canada

He stood there like an African prince, majestic in his wrath, as with wit, satire, and indignation he graphically described the bitterness of slavery and the humiliation of subjection to those who . . . were inferior to himself. Thus it was that I first saw Frederick Douglass, and wondered that any mortal man should have ever tried to subjugate a being with such talents, intensified with the love of liberty.

Elizabeth Cady Stanton, on first seeing Frederick Douglass at an abolitionist meeting in the 1840s

CONTENTS

Gold-knobbed cane presented to Douglass in the 1890s by the Wayman Grove Camp Meeting Association. Frederick Douglass Papers, Moorland-Spingarn Research Center, Howard University, Washington, D.C.

LENDERS TO THE EXHIBITION

Anacostia Museum, Smithsonian Institution, Washington, D.C.

The Trustees of the Boston Public Library, Massachusetts

Clements Library, The University of Michigan, Ann Arbor

The Gelman Library, The George Washington University, Washington, D.C.

Jerome C. Gray

Ronald L. Harris

Houghton Library, Harvard University, Cambridge, Massachusetts

Library Company of Philadelphia, Pennsylvania

Library of Congress, Washington, D.C.

Madison County Historical Society, Oneida, New York

Moorland-Spingarn Research Center, Howard University, Washington, D.C.

National Museum of American History, Smithsonian Institution, Washington, D.C.

National Park Service, United States Department of the Interior, Washington, D.C.

National Portrait Gallery, Smithsonian Institution, Washington, D.C.

New Bedford Whaling Museum, Massachusetts

The New York Public Library, New York City

Providence Public Library, Rhode Island

Schomburg Center for Research in Black Culture, The New York Public Library, New York City

Smith College, Northampton, Massachusetts

State Historical Society of Wisconsin, Madison

Syracuse University Library, New York

Frederick Douglass in his thirties

Unidentified photographer

Daguerreotype, 8.3 × 7 cm (3¹/₄ × 2³/₄ in.), circa 1850–1855

William Rubel

FOREWORD
The Enduring Frederick Douglass

In this year—1995—the centennial of the death of Frederick Douglass, it is appropriate that we, as a nation, reflect on his continuing meaning for America. We are still grappling mightily with two intertwined issues that deeply concerned the youthful United States in the nineteenth century: race and the country's self-image. Douglass was equally proud to be American and an African American. As a result, he dedicated himself to helping his people—both Americans generally and African Americans specifically—resolve the tension between race and nation.

His enduring legacy forces us to think anew about the centrality of this historic tension between identities of race and nation. Pointedly rejecting the concept of the United States as a "white" or racially exclusive country, Douglass envisioned a broadly inclusive America transcending narrow and divisive boundaries like race. For all of our talk in late-twentieth-century America about our multicultural nation and our ethnic and racial diversity, as a nation we have far to go if we are to commit ourselves to realizing the broadly inclusive national self-image so dear to Douglass.

He often spoke of the United States as a "composite nationality." This vision skillfully blended its constituent peoples and their cultures into a rich and stimulating mosaic. On one hand, this nineteenth-century version of multiculturalism sought to enhance commonalities and unity. On the other, this pluralist view of the United States vigorously embraced differences, minorities, and alternative positions. Douglass's visionary spirit led him to fight his entire life for a better world, as well as a better America. As we tackle the problems of the twenty-first century, we should continue to revitalize this invigorating legacy.

Douglass's memory speaks so forcefully to us today precisely because it calls forth the primacy of understanding the African American experience for comprehending our national experience. The fundamental historical reality that African Americans have been central to the origins and development of the American nation structured Douglass's view of the national experience.

For him, the national heritage thus necessarily encompassed the essential contributions of African Americans.

Equally important, the national heritage also necessarily encompassed the deep-seated tragedy of white freedom built upon black slavery. Over time, Americans have increasingly come to understand what Douglass himself understood so well and endeavored to impress upon the nation's conscience: the destructive human impact of antiblack racism and discrimination. Invoking the spirit of those like Douglass, perhaps in the last years of the twentieth century we can truly renew the difficult battle to alleviate all forms of racism and discrimination.

Persistent patterns of black subordination in various guises—including enslavement, sharecropping, terrorism, imprisonment, Jim Crow—have clearly been tied inextricably to white self-definition, white liberty, and white advancement. Thus, the historical logic of Douglass's line of argument confirms that denying blacks the vote for most of this nation's history was as much about creating and sustaining a sense of identity and unity among different white ethnic groups and classes as it was about degrading and exploiting blacks. Douglass explained, moreover, that a significant portion of this nation's wealth—in effect white wealth—has come from the unpaid labor of African American slaves and the underpaid labor of free African Americans. If we are ever to deal justly with the complex historical patterns of white dominance and black subordination, we must—as Douglass demanded in the nineteenth century—fully comprehend those patterns.

The African American liberation struggle that Douglass personified, however, was ultimately far more about nurturance, affirmation, and creation—"making a way where there was no way." The oppression and degradation that blacks endured strengthened their resolve to be free and equal citizens of a nation which they, too, envisioned and built. It is this progressive and hopeful vision that best captures how Douglass preferred to see his own life, the history of African Americans, and the history of all Americans. Indeed, America was an exceptional place under God's guidance, according to this commonly held view. Here, in this most uncommon world, the prospects for social reform made human perfectibility appear possible.

It was this kind of romantic faith in America as a place of unusual promise that combined with Douglass's own extraordinary abilities and good fortune to enable him to become a remarkable yet representative American. From the humblest of origins and against great odds—born a slave in Tuckahoe, Maryland, in 1818—Douglass rose to dizzying heights. He escaped to freedom in 1838 and began his spectacular ascent to greatness. Quite appropriately, in his last years he lived at Cedar Hill, a hilltop estate in southeast Washington, D.C., with a breathtaking view of the capital area. He had come "a mighty long way."

His noteworthy achievements as race leader, abolitionist, orator, journalist, author, social reformer, political activist, and Republican Party advocate established him as a commanding presence. Those achievements actively advanced his nation's efforts to actualize its ideals of freedom, equality, and justice for all. The living memory of Douglass—and monumental figures like him—helps to sustain the ongoing struggles of the American nation to realize its best self. In this sense, it is essential to understand Douglass's continuing importance as a world citizen and an American advocate.

The primary basis for Douglass's emergence as a powerful exponent of the best of American ideals was his tireless work on behalf of African American freedom. He was without question the most important African American leader and personality of the nineteenth century. In fact, Douglass was such a thoroughly compelling voice in the national and international movements to end African American chattel slavery that for countless numbers he came to embody the American abolitionist movement. His uncanny ability, as a brilliant ex-slave, to articulate insightfully slavery's unconscionable wrongs authenticated his authority and increased his influence.

His autobiographies—*Narrative of the Life of Frederick Douglass, An American Slave* (1845), *My Bondage and My Freedom* (1855); *Life and Times of Frederick Douglass* (1881; revised 1892)—recount a captivating life story and help explain why he remains a powerful symbol for our times as well as his own. That he accomplished so much after having started from such a lowly station only enhanced the measure of his success and respectability. This progressive view of Douglass's life exemplifies the ideal of America as the land of hope for all, even the former slaves. The grand narrative of Douglass's life—an American success story whose hero is the epitome of the American self-made man—reveals enormous inspirational and symbolic power.

He fought ceaselessly to awaken his nation's and the world's conscience to the African American freedom struggle as a two-pronged battle, both to make African Americans first-class citizens and to free the slaves. In *My Bondage and My Freedom* (in many ways his most revealing autobiography), he wrote so movingly about the imperative of ridding the nation of the awful prejudice and discrimination that free African Americans confronted because he also experienced the same dreadful curses. As Douglass saw the African American freedom struggle, therefore, it was as much about abolishing racism as it was about abolishing slavery. Indeed, in his view, these battles were inseparable.

When Douglass died on the evening of February 20, 1895, he bequeathed to all Americans, but particularly to African Americans, an exceptional legacy of human-rights advocacy. On the afternoon of his death, he had attended a meeting of the pro-women's-rights Woman's Council. In fact, Douglass was a pathbreaking and influential supporter of the nineteenth-century women's rights movement. The masthead of his antebellum newspaper the *North Star* once read: "Right is of no sex." His lifelong commitment to equality was deep and abiding. That intensely humanistic commitment remains highly instructive.

During his lifetime, Douglass saw the United States go through many fundamental changes: urbanization, immigration, industrialization, Civil War, and Reconstruction. For him, however, all of these changes paled in significance next to his people's emancipation during the Civil War. Particularly meaningful for Douglass were the crucial efforts of countless slaves to free themselves—not just as soldiers but in various and sundry ways amid the war's turbulence.

Never forgetting those moments of unspeakable joy when his people realized their freedom, Douglass maintained his bedrock faith in America's promise. That undying faith sustained him during the bleakest days of his later life, as America increasingly reneged on its promises of full freedom, justice, and equality to its African American citizens. The key to a better world, Douglass always proclaimed, was firm commitment and constant struggle, especially in the worst of times. In our cynical and postmodern age, we would do well to heed Douglass's classic admonition of the critical need for ongoing social struggle. As he once so eloquently observed: "If there is no struggle, there is no progress."

WALDO E. MARTIN, JR.
PROFESSOR OF HISTORY
University of California, Berkeley

INTRODUCTION

On February 21, 1895, the newspapers in Washington, D.C., announced the death of Frederick Douglass. He had died the night before at his home on Cedar Hill. The next day, February 22, the Washington *Evening Star* ran a feature article of reminiscences from Douglass's contemporaries. Some were lighthearted, others were more serious, but all were in agreement that one of America's transcendent figures was gone. After his death, Douglass's legacy remained as a powerful force in the African American community, with a number of organizations and companies named in his honor. Yet many of the major works on American history either briefly mentioned his name or omitted it altogether.

In 1948, however, the noted historian Benjamin Quarles redefined Douglass's prominence with his highly regarded biography. Two years later, Philip S. Foner added to the awareness of Douglass when he began the publication of a four-volume collection of his significant papers and speeches. In 1979 John W. Blassingame began the publication of the complete collection of Douglass's writings and speeches. Other biographies and studies began to appear. Then, in 1991, the Pulitzer Prize–winning scholar William S. McFeely wrote *Frederick Douglass,* a thorough and eloquent biography of this American leader. A number of other recent books, articles, and films have focused on Douglass as well. Today, it would be unthinkable for anyone to write a serious study or produce a film documenting the antislavery movement, the Civil War, or major African American leaders without giving Douglass a prominent place.

The exhibition "Majestic in His Wrath: The Life of Frederick Douglass" commemorates one of America's major figures, bringing together many of the most significant images, speeches, writings, and objects associated with his life. Spanning Douglass's humble origins in slavery, through his prominent role in the abolitionist movement, to his positions of influence within the Republican Party, we see a remarkably brilliant, passionate, and complex man. In a period of history that produced many truly great reformers, Douglass stands out as one of the most compelling; in an era where hour-long, spell-

On her last visit with him, Douglass's mother chastises a slave cook for her meanness to her son. Engraving from *Life and Times of Frederick Douglass* (1881)

binding orations were the norm, Douglass's speeches were among the most eloquent. And during an age when most African Americans were relegated—at best—to subservient roles and—at worst—to slavery, Douglass emerged as one of the most respected leaders of his day.

Americans have always been fascinated by individuals who lift themselves from extreme poverty or disadvantage to achieve success. Horatio Alger sold more than 200 million books following the Civil War by focusing on characters such as "Ragged Dick" or "Poorhouse Jed," who used their pluck to overcome incredible odds to succeed in life. In contrast, Frederick Douglass's story was real, and far more remarkable than any of Alger's fictitious tales. In fact, of all the leaders in American history, few started from such humble origins and ended by reaching such heights as Frederick Douglass.

He was born to a slave mother—whom he rarely saw after his birth—sometime in February of 1818 on the Eastern Shore of Maryland. The identity of his white father was never revealed to him. He spent his early life in slavery on Eastern Shore plantations and in Baltimore. Douglass escaped from his bondage on September 3, 1838, and married Anna Murray, a free-black woman who had helped him plot his escape. Settling in New Bedford, Massachusetts, he engaged in a number of odd jobs and became active in a local African American church. At several public meetings he spoke out against the evils of slavery and gradually drew the attention of prominent New England abolitionists. Then, in August of 1841, Douglass was invited to speak before the Massachusetts Anti-Slavery Society's summer meeting at Nantucket. Later he would say that because he was so nervous, he could not exactly recall anything that he had said. Even so, this speech catapulted him into the limelight as one of the strongest weapons in the antislavery arsenal.

The Massachusetts society immediately recruited Douglass on its lecture circuit to give his firsthand account of the evils of slavery. Responding to writers who claimed that so eloquent a man could not have spent his early life in slavery, Douglass published the first version of his autobiography, *Narrative of the Life of Frederick Douglass,* in 1845. In this volume, he dispassionately recounted the horrors of slavery. He also lashed out at the hypocrisy of the slave owners who professed Christian piety yet beat and sold their human

Douglass's first pocket watch, purchased during his tour of the British Isles in 1845–1847

Frederick Douglass Papers, Moorland-Spingarn Research Center, Howard University, Washington, D.C.

chattels and sired biracial children, who remained in slavery. Within five years, the *Narrative* had sold more than 30,000 copies.

The popularity of Douglass's autobiography increased the risk of his capture and return to slavery. Thus, in 1845 he left the United States for an extended visit to the British Isles, where he lectured extensively about the plight of American slaves. Much to his surprise, the new friends he made there arranged to purchase his freedom. When Douglass returned to the United States in 1847, he decided to embark upon a new career as editor and publisher of an antislavery newspaper, the *North Star*. He launched his venture in Rochester, New York, which became his home for the next twenty-odd years.

Douglass continued as a lecturer, and his oratorical strength remained a major force in the battle against slavery. In perhaps his most powerful speech—delivered on July 5, 1852, in Rochester—Douglass proclaimed that slaves in particular, and African Americans in general, found it impossible to participate in Fourth of July celebrations. "There is not a nation on the earth guilty of practices more shocking and bloody," he stated, "than are the people of these United States, at this very hour." One of the consequences of the country's long-standing tolerance for slavery, he charged, was that "America reign[ed] supreme" in the world for its "revolting barbarity and shameless hypocrisy."

In 1855 Douglass expanded his autobiography in a new version, entitled *My Bondage and My Freedom*. Rather than simply revising his earlier work, Douglass crafted a more thorough story of his life. For example, in the *Narrative* he only briefly mentioned the beating his aunt received at the hands of her owner; but in *Bondage*, he increased the description to several pages, detailing the sadism inherent in the American slavery system.

In both versions, Douglass had the singular purpose of presenting the evils of slavery to the public. Thus, he omitted many important events in his life. For example, he did not describe his involvement in the Seneca Falls Convention of 1848, the first major meeting focusing on the rights of American women. Douglass, in partnership with Elizabeth Cady Stanton, gave his full support to the Declaration of Sentiments, which demanded equal suffrage for women. With this action, Douglass demonstrated that his fight for equality went well beyond defending the rights of his fellow African Americans.

As the Civil War began, Douglass directed his talents and energy toward ensuring that the abolition of slavery was an aim of the war. When Abraham Lincoln's Emancipation Proclamation of January 1, 1863, accomplished that goal, Douglass redirected his efforts to recruiting enlistments for the all-black Fifty-fourth Massachusetts Volunteers. In addition to traveling far and wide to seek recruits, he used his periodical, *Douglass' Monthly*, to call "Men of Color to Arms." Two of his sons, Lewis and Charles, joined the Fifty-fourth. In all, Douglass helped to raise two regiments of African American soldiers (about 2,000 individuals) to fight in the Civil War.

Douglass was sometimes irritated with Lincoln's wartime policies, but in his two White House meetings with Lincoln, Douglass found him immensely personable. At one of these meetings, while Douglass was in Lincoln's office, the President's secretary interrupted to say that the governor of Connecticut had arrived for his scheduled appointment. Lincoln asked the secretary to inform the governor that he wanted "to have a long meeting with his friend Frederick Douglass" and that the governor would simply need to wait. Douglass later reflected that this probably was the first time in the history of the United States that the chief executive "exercise[d] such an act of impartiality between persons so widely different in their positions and supposed claims upon his attention."

Douglass believed that Lincoln provided the best hope for the future of African Americans. Thus, he was devastated by the news of Lincoln's assassination. Douglass's devotion to the fallen President was recognized when he was invited, in 1876, to deliver the major address at the dedication of Lincoln's Emancipation Monument in Lincoln Square on Capitol Hill. This statue was erected largely with funds donated by former slaves, and the dedication ceremony was attended by President Ulysses S. Grant, his cabinet, members of the Supreme Court, and members of Congress.

After the war, Douglass believed that the right to vote offered the best means for freed slaves to enter the mainstream of American life. Thus he be-

Douglass spent his last years at Cedar Hill, a residence that he purchased in 1877, which was located in a section of Washington, D.C., known today as Anacostia. Made into a museum after his death, the house itself was comfortably large but by no means grand. However, its spacious, well-kept grounds and its setting—on top of a hill that commanded an impressive view of the nation's capital—invested Cedar Hill with a seignorial splendor.

Unidentified photographer
Prints and Photographs Department, Moorland-Spingarn Research Center, Howard University, Washington, D.C.

came an ardent supporter of the passage of the Fifteenth Amendment. He also viewed the Republican Party—the party of Lincoln and slave emancipation—as the best protector of the welfare of African Americans. As Douglass became more involved in politics, the power of the nation's capital drew him in, and in 1872 he left his long-term residence in Rochester and moved to Washington, D.C.

When he arrived in Washington, Douglass believed that the Republican Party would continue to enact beneficial measures for African American people. After 1877, however, the Republicans' commitment to Reconstruction waned dramatically, with the consequent steady erosion of many of the post–Civil War advances experienced by blacks. Yet Douglass's support for the party remained intact, and he vigorously supported its presidential candidates through 1888. His loyalty was rewarded with appointments as United States marshal and recorder of deeds for the District of Columbia, and as minister to Haiti.

In 1878 Douglass purchased a fine estate, Cedar Hill, on a prominent knoll east of the Anacostia River, overlooking the Capitol. Then, in 1881, he embarked on writing yet another version of his autobiography. *The Life and Times of Frederick Douglass* would again tell the story of his life in slavery, but here he would also include his association with John Brown, his experiences during the Civil War—including his meetings with Abraham Lincoln—and his life after the war. Although the passion and immediacy of his earlier autobiographies were missing, he presented his entire life in the context of the times in which he lived.

A year after he wrote *Life and Times,* Anna Murray Douglass, his wife of more than forty years, died. Within two years, he married Helen Pitts, a white woman. While he lived in relative comfort on Cedar Hill, his goals for his people became increasingly difficult to achieve due to growing national indifference. His passion for justice, however, remained intact. In his last major address, "The Lessons of the Hour," on January 9, 1894, at the Metropolitan African Methodist Episcopal Church in Washington, D.C., he vented his concerns for African Americans with the same oratorical fervor of his earlier antislavery speeches. He lashed out at the appalling increase of lynchings in the South and the refusal of the authorities to take any action. Furthermore, he criticized the Supreme Court for dismembering the Civil Rights Act and also disparaged the Republican Party, which he had revered for so long, for becoming "a party of money rather than a party of morals."

In 1892 he revised *Life and Times* as a final retrospective on his life. In concluding this version of his autobiography, Douglass wrote: "Contemplating my life as a whole, I have to say that, although it has at times been dark and stormy, and I have met with hardships from which other men have been exempted, yet my life has in many respects been remarkably full of sunshine and joy." Thus, taken as whole, Frederick Douglass could look back at the suffering of his early life in slavery, the retreat of the Republican Party from its Reconstruction program, and the affronts of racial prejudice, and through it all he could still view his life in a positive light.

Through the efforts of a number of groups and individuals, Frederick Douglass has returned to the place of prominence he so richly deserves. Shortly after his death, Helen Pitts Douglass established the Frederick Douglass Memorial and Historical Association to perpetuate the memory of her husband. She further designated that Cedar Hill and all of Douglass's possessions should be managed by the association as a monument to him. In 1916 the National Association of Colored Women's Clubs joined the association in operating the home as a museum. In 1952 the memorial association arranged for the construction of a low- and moderate-income apartment complex on a portion of the estate to help support the maintenance of Cedar Hill. Then, in 1962, the Frederick Douglass Home was turned over to the federal government as a unit of the National Park Service. Today the Park Service manages the home as a National Historic Site. The housing units are currently owned by the Frederick Douglass Housing Corporation. Cedar Hill is open to the public every day except January 1, Thanksgiving, and December 25.

In 1926 the Association for the Study of Afro-American Life and History, under the direction of Dr. Carter G. Woodson, established "Negro History Week" to coincide with the week in February in which Frederick Douglass and Abraham Lincoln were born. In 1976 the celebration was expanded to "Black History Month," accompanied with a presidential proclamation. More recently, in 1994, a Pulitzer Prize was awarded to *Washington Post* columnist William Raspberry. His entry included a column that began, "What would Frederick Douglass say . . . now?" In this personalized essay, Raspberry noted that Douglass would be pleased by the many advances of African Americans. The top military leader in the country at the time was a black man, as was the governor of Virginia. But the columnist further speculated that Douglass would likely be heartbroken with the poverty, crime, drugs, and despair experienced by many inner-city African Americans.

In the century following Douglass's death, African Americans have indeed experienced remarkable progress. The downside described by William Raspberry is equally troubling. Yet Frederick Douglass's legacy leaves some hope for future generations. He was born into the most desperate situation imaginable, but he achieved remarkable heights with his intelligence, ingenuity, and tenacity. His life, and the impressive volume of writings and speeches he left behind, offer inspiration to all people today. We hope the exhibition will perpetuate the story and the lessons of this truly great man.

ROBERT K. SUTTON
ASSISTANT SUPERINTENDENT
National Capital Parks-East, National Park Service

Under the whole heavens there is no relation more unfavorable to the development of honorable character, than that sustained by the slaveholder to the slave. Reason is imprisoned here, and passions run wild. Like the fires of the prairie, once lighted, they are at the mercy of every wind, and must burn, till they have consumed all that is combustible within their remorseless grasp.

Frederick Douglass,
My Bondage and My Freedom (1855)

BEGINNINGS IN SLAVERY

When Frederick Douglass took the abolitionist platform to denounce the evils of slavery in the early 1840s, he could claim intimate familiarity with his subject. Born a slave on Maryland's Eastern Shore, he had in his first twenty years of life both observed and experienced a host of deprivations and cruelties that were so often integral to the daily pattern of the South's slave system. He knew, for example, what it was like to grow up separated from his mother and then be unexpectedly wrenched from his grandmother at the age of six. He knew the pangs of hunger that came with being denied sufficient food. Finally, he knew about living in fear of physical punishment for the slightest offense, or even for mishaps clearly beyond his control. Throughout his adult life, he would carry scars on his back testifying to a number of brutal lashings administered by one of his taskmasters.

But to some extent, Douglass's owners consciously spared him from some of slavery's harsher realities, eventually placing the young man in circumstances that allowed him to teach himself to read and write. By his late teens, he was living in Baltimore, where his surrogate master briefly permitted him to hire himself out for wages, a portion of which he could keep for his own use.

Yet these advantages only deepened Douglass's resentment of slavery and strengthened his resolve to seek refuge from his bondsman's lot in the North. By his twentieth birthday, the only question left unanswered about his flight was when it would take place.

Young Frederick Douglass witnesses the beating of a fellow slave. Engraving from *Life and Times of Frederick Douglass* (1881)

Wye House, where Douglass spent part of his boyhood

Photograph by H. Robins Hollyday
H. Robins Hollyday Collection, Historical
Society of Talbot County, Easton, Maryland

Born Frederick Bailey, Douglass spent his first years of life in the care of his maternal grandmother, a slave midwife who lived with her freeman husband in a cabin somewhat removed from the working slave communities of surrounding farms. As a result, Douglass did not begin to learn about slavery until he was brought to Wye House at age six. Located in Talbot County, Maryland, Wye House stood at the center of a vast and thriving agricultural fiefdom owned by Edward Lloyd and managed by Douglass's original owner, Aaron Anthony. There, the boy first glimpsed his future as a slave.

Writing of this initiation years later, Douglass confessed, "I have nothing cruel or shocking to relate of my own personal experience." Indeed, the tasks assigned him at Wye House were relatively light, and his punishment for wrongdoing did not go beyond "an occasional cuff" from a mean-spirited slave cook or a whipping from "old master, such as any . . . mischievous boy might get from his father." Nevertheless, Douglass learned quickly about slavery's darker side. During his two-year stay at Wye House, he both saw and heard about cruelties visited on the adult slaves around him, which ranged from brutal beatings to murder.

Douglass's owner, Thomas Auld

Courtesy Mrs. William Sears

When Douglass was eight, his original owner, Aaron Anthony, died, and in the division of his estate, Douglass became the property of Anthony's son-in-law, Thomas Auld.

Douglass would later portray Auld as a man "incapable of a noble action," who was driven by "intense selfishness" and "love of domination." Later, as an antislavery crusader, he charged Auld with committing all manner of cruelties. In their specificity of detail, these denunciations were a wonderfully effective vehicle for dramatizing the evils of slavery. They were not, however, particularly accurate. While Auld had his moments of harsh callousness, he could also be unusually compassionate and tolerant. The best evidence of this was his reaction to Douglass's failed conspiracy with other slaves to escape to the North in 1836. Many slaveholders would have retaliated by shipping off the troublesome Douglass for sale in the Deep South, where the slave's lot was considerably harder than on Maryland's Eastern Shore. Instead, Auld sent him to a brother in Baltimore, where Douglass had considerably more latitude in regulating his life, and his opportunities for escape were vastly enlarged. Thus, whatever else this decision suggested about Auld's character, it was not indicative of an irredeemably cruel and self-serving nature. More likely, the decision was a reflection of real concern for Douglass's welfare.

Alexander Rider (lifedates unknown), for Kennedy and Lucas Lithography Company
Lithograph, 32.7 × 48 cm (12 7/8 × 18 7/8 in.), 1829
Prints and Photographs Division, Library of Congress, Washington, D.C.

An early nineteenth-century religious revival meeting

During the 1820s and 1830s, a regular event in America's rural culture was the religious revival, such as the one pictured here, where, in response to an onslaught of emotionally charged preaching, people embraced Christianity with renewed and deepened fervor. In his mid-teens, Douglass briefly placed great hope for himself and other slaves in these gatherings. It seemed only reasonable that any slaveholder who came away from a revival with a strengthened commitment to Christianity would immediately free his slaves or, at the very least, treat them more generously. Unfortunately, that was generally not the case, and after a revival rekindled the Christian faith of his master, Thomas Auld, in 1833, Douglass noted that the new religiosity brought no improvement whatsoever for Auld's slaves.

Douglass's disillusionment with religion's power to ease his plight as a slave became all but complete in 1834, when Auld leased him out to a nearby farmer named Edward Covey. Under the fearsomely demanding Covey, Douglass suffered the harshest treatment that he would ever experience as a slave. Yet this man who routinely brutalized his slaves, Douglass noted, was deeply religious. When it came to prayer, Bible-reading, and churchgoing, no one observed these outward expressions of Christian piety more rigorously than Covey.

American Slave Market

This painting depicts a scene that embodied the worst nightmare for Douglass and other Upper South slaves—being suddenly torn from all that was familiar, placed on the auction block, and sold to a cotton planter in the Deep South. Although the life of a Maryland slave could be difficult, stories floating up from farther south indicated that conditions were harder yet for field hands on cotton plantations in Mississippi, Georgia, and Alabama. What was more, by putting the slave at a substantially greater distance from the free North, relocation to the Deep South shut off virtually all chances for escape from that harsher existence.

The specter of being "sold south" weighed particularly heavily on Douglass, because as he advanced through his teens, he increasingly showed unwillingness to accept some of the conditions of his bondage. And that made him an especially ripe candidate for being shipped off to the "living death" of a Deep South cotton field. Nothing was more likely to prompt the sale of a Maryland slave than a reputation for rebelliousness.

Taylor (lifedates unknown)
Oil on canvas, 71.4 × 85.7 cm
(28 $^1/_8$ × 33 $^3/_4$ in.), circa 1855
Chicago Historical Society, Illinois

View of Baltimore dating from Douglass's residence there

William J. Bennett (1784–1844)
Colored aquatint, 42.1 × 61.4 cm
(16 ⁹/₁₆ × 24 ³/₁₆ in.), 1831
I. N. Phelps Stokes Collection, The
Miriam and Ira D. Wallach Division of Arts, Prints and Photographs, The New York Public Library, Astor, Lenox and Tilden Foundations, New York City

Douglass spent nearly ten of his last thirteen years in slavery living with his second owner's brother, Hugh Auld, in Baltimore. Life in this urban center of the Upper South was eminently preferable to that of his native Eastern Shore. Here, though still very much a slave who had to answer to his surrogate master, he enjoyed substantially more freedom, had better housing and food, and ultimately found himself set to work in local shipyards, where his tasks were considerably less onerous than they would have been back on the farms of the Eastern Shore. For awhile in 1838, Auld even permitted him to live independently, provided that Douglass turn over to him a set amount of his weekly wages.

Life, however, was not so idyllic that Douglass could ever forget one unsettling fact: He was still a slave whose fate rested on the whims of others, a reality that, regardless of his easy situation, he ultimately could not live with.

Douglass's copy of *The Columbian Orator*

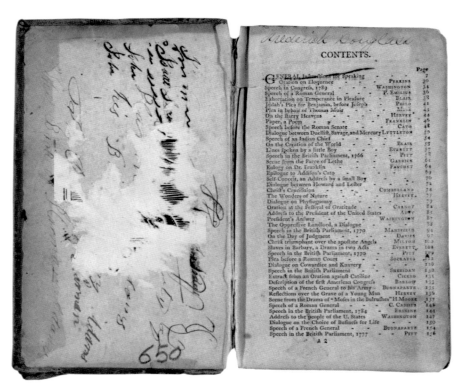

CONTENTS.

National Park Service, Frederick Douglass
National Historic Site, Washington, D.C.

While living in Baltimore with his owner's brother and sister-in-law, Hugh and Sophia Auld, Douglass received some reading instruction from Sophia. Owing to her husband's disapproval of educating slaves, the lessons did not go on for long. But they gave Douglass the impetus to secretly pursue a regimen of self-education. Guided by a discarded speller and by old copybook exercises of the Aulds' son, he was soon mastering the basics of reading and writing.

At the age of thirteen, ready for greater challenges, Douglass obtained a copy of *The Columbian Orator,* a collection of orations, poems, and dialogues designed to encourage the reader's verbal eloquence and virtue. Purchased with money earned from shining boots, the *Orator* was an epiphany for Douglass on two counts. First, the book's high-minded regard for personal liberty made him aware for the first time that there was a significant body of organized thought holding slavery to be morally wrong. Second, the *Orator*'s selection of famous speeches inspired Douglass to perfect his own oratorical powers, and he spent hours absorbing the book's hints on speaking mannerisms, which would later shape his early platform style on the abolitionist circuit.

John Quincy Adams   1767–1848

About 1830, Douglass began overhearing white Marylanders angrily blaming discipline problems among their slaves on dissatisfactions bred by something called the "abolition movement." For a long time, he could not figure out what this term meant, and resort to a dictionary helped very little. But thanks to former President John Quincy Adams, who was just beginning his first term in the House of Representatives, the mystery was finally solved. In late 1831, the *Baltimore American* reported that Adams had presented fifteen popular petitions in the House, demanding the outlawing of slavery in the District of Columbia. Throughout its account, the newspaper had linked the word "abolition" to slavery. When Douglass read this item, suddenly the contemporary significance of abolition was crystal clear. More important, it dawned on this thirteen-year-old bondsman that, outside of his immediate world in Maryland, a movement was afoot to unmask the "rascality of slaveholders," and in that he found great hope.

Eastman Johnson (1824–1906)
Crayon on paper, 54.6 × 39.4 cm
(21 ¹/₂ × 15 ¹/₂ in.), 1846
National Portrait Gallery, Smithsonian
Institution, Washington, D.C.

Portrayal of Douglass escaping from slavery

In the spring of 1838, Douglass's surrogate master, Hugh Auld, granted him the privilege of hiring himself out for wages in Baltimore's shipyards, provided Douglass give Auld part of his weekly earnings. This liberal arrangement also allowed Douglass to live independently and to retain for his own use whatever of his wages was left over after paying Auld and meeting his room-and-board expenses. But when Douglass was a little late in one of his payments to Auld, the latter angrily retaliated by forcing Douglass to return to a more tightly constrained master-slave relationship.

Auld's revocation of Douglass's quasi-freedom was the final straw. Long determined to have his total freedom one day, Douglass began hatching plans for his escape to the North with Anna Murray, a young free-black domestic servant in Baltimore with whom he had formed an intimate attachment. On September 3, 1838, affecting the clothes and manner of an experienced sailor bound to sea and carrying a false document implying that he was legally free, Douglass nervously boarded a train in Baltimore. In less than twenty-four hours, he was in New York City, where by prearrangement he met and married Anna. Shortly thereafter, as extra insurance against recapture, he exchanged his original surname, Bailey, for Douglass, a name inspired by Sir Walter Scott's heroine, Ellen Douglas, in *Lady of the Lake*.

Henry Prentiss, publisher
Lithograph, 35.5 × 27.3 cm (14 × 10 3/4 in.), 1845
Library Company of Philadelphia, Pennsylvania

THE FUGITIVE'S SONG,

WORDS

composed and respectfully dedicated in token of confidential esteem to

FREDERICK DOUGLASS

A Graduate from the
"PECULIAR INSTITUTION"

For his fearless advocacy signal ability and wonderful success in behalf of

HIS BROTHERS IN BONDS.
FUGITIVES FROM SLAVERY
FREE STATES & CANADAS.

by their friend

JESSE HUTCHINSON JUN.ᵣ

BOSTON Published by HENRY PRENTISS 33 Court St.

View of New Bedford from the Fort near Fairhaven
Fitz Hugh Lane (1804–1865), after A. Conant
Lithograph, 41.6 × 64.1 cm (16 ³/8 × 25 ¹/4 in.), 1845
New Bedford Whaling Museum, Massachusetts

New Bedford, Massachusetts, where Douglass began his life of freedom

Following their flight from Maryland, Douglass and his new wife, Anna, settled in New Bedford, Massachusetts. They could not have chosen a better place to begin their new life. A center of New England's whaling industry, New Bedford was the richest city per capita in America. More important, it had a thriving African American community anxious to aid Douglass in getting a start, as well as many abolitionist-minded whites ready to join their black townsmen in preventing any slave-catcher from restoring Douglass to his Maryland owner. Among New Bedford's most startling pluses for someone accustomed to the mores of southern racism was the revelation that white and black children attended the same schools. Douglass was shocked almost beyond belief when also told that a black man might, if so inclined, seek public office.

But Douglass soon learned that although he had had much experience as a ship's caulker in Baltimore, the color of his skin shut him out of that trade in New Bedford. Instead, during his first year there, he was forced to seek unskilled work at wages far below those of a caulker. Nevertheless, New Bedford struck the newly arrived Douglass as about as close to an earthly paradise as any onetime slave was likely to encounter.

The existence of slavery in this country brands your republicanism as a sham, your humanity as a base pretense and your Christianity as a lie. . . . It fetters your progress; it is the enemy of improvement; the deadly foe of education; it fosters pride; it breeds insolence, it promotes vice; it shelters crime; it is a curse to the earth that supports it; and yet you cling to it as if it were the sheet anchor of all your hopes.

Frederick Douglass,
"What to the Slave Is the Fourth of July?"
July 5, 1852

SPOKESMAN FOR ABOLITION

Once Douglass settled into his life in New Bedford, it was inevitable that he should be drawn into the orbit of the town's substantial contingent of anti-slavery activists. By early 1839, he was participating regularly in local abolitionist gatherings, where his concrete testimonies to the oppressions of slavery held enormous interest for listeners who understood slavery's evils only in the abstract. Two years later, this modest involvement set off a chain of events that would make him the most influential African American of his time.

Invited to attend a convention of the Massachusetts Anti-Slavery Society on Nantucket in August 1841, Douglass arrived in this island community, regarding his stay there largely as a pleasant respite from his daily toils as a manual laborer. But the holiday spirit gave way to stage fright on August 16, when he consented to a spur-of-the-moment request that he speak about his slave experience before the whole convention. Pulling himself together "with the utmost difficulty," Douglass later recalled, he nervously stammered through his remarks. Yet the halting delivery could not conceal his gifts for public persuasion. By the time Douglass left Nantucket, he had agreed to put those gifts to the test as a traveling lecturer for the antislavery movement.

To describe this shift in vocation as successful would be an understatement. It was soon clear that Douglass's flair for oratory was considerable indeed, and within a few years, his rich, full voice, majestic delivery, and original blend of humor and moral urgency had transformed him into one of the most compelling speakers on the abolitionist circuit. Describing the figure Douglass cut at an antislavery gathering in 1849, a journalist warned readers that it was hard to overrate his effectiveness. "He is a swarthy Ajax," declared the reporter, "and with ponderous mace, he springs into the midst of his white oppressors and crushes them at every blow. With an air of scorn he hurls his bolts on every hand. . . . [He] is the master of every weapon. His powers of ridicule are great. Woe to the man . . . whose hypocrisy passes in review."

Douglass confronts opponents to abolition at an antislavery meeting in Indiana. Engraving from *Life and Times of Frederick Douglass* (1881)

Frederick Douglass at an outdoor abolitionist meeting

In his early years as an antislavery speaker, Douglass was advised to limit his content to a simple narrative of the wrongs he had seen and experienced as a slave, and to let the more educated abolitionist orators illuminate his recitation with abstract moralizing about slavery's evil. He was further counseled to retain "a *little* of the plantation" in his speech patterns to reinforce his believability. Initially Douglass accepted these guidelines. But as time passed, he grew restive with playing the role of a simple ex-slave, and his denunciations of slavery started taking on a substantially greater intellectual sophistication and polish.

In the daguerreotype here, Douglass is seen seated *(center right)* on a platform at an abolitionist gathering in Cazenovia, New York, in August 1850. The man standing just behind him is Gerrit Smith, one of Douglass's main financial supporters for his rarely solvent antislavery newspaper, the *North Star.*

Ezra Greenleaf Weld (lifedates unknown)
Daguerreotype, 14 × 11.4 cm (5 ¹/₂ × 4 ¹/₂
    in.), 1850
Madison County Historical Society, Oneida,
    New York

Douglass in his late twenties

Completed sometime between 1841 and 1845, this likeness is a visual testament to Douglass's enormous value to the antislavery cause. As an observer at one of Douglass's abolitionist appearances in 1842 put it, this "fine specimen of an orator," who invited favorable comparisons with no less than Daniel Webster, was "a living, speaking, *startling* proof of the folly, absurdity and inconsistency . . . of slavery."

Unidentified artist
Oil on canvas, 69.9 × 57.2 cm (27 1/2 × 22 1/2 in.), circa 1845
National Portrait Gallery, Smithsonian Institution, Washington, D.C.

Early edition of *Narrative of the Life of Frederick Douglass, an American Slave,* 1845

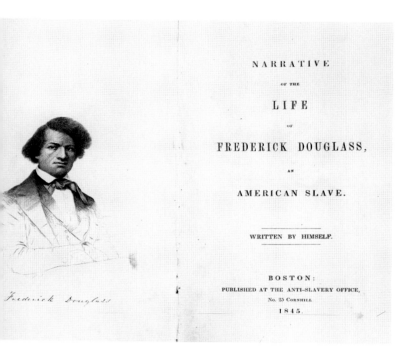

NARRATIVE

OF THE

LIFE

OF

FREDERICK DOUGLASS,

AN

AMERICAN SLAVE.

WRITTEN BY HIMSELF.

BOSTON:
PUBLISHED AT THE ANTI-SLAVERY OFFICE,
No. 25 CORNHILL
1845.

During his first years as an abolitionist speaker, Douglass carefully refrained from revealing many details of his life in slavery. The reason for this reticence was obvious: If, for instance, he told audiences where he had been born and disclosed that his name in slavery had been Frederick Bailey, he would have vastly increased the chance of being forced to return to his Maryland owners. But as Douglass lost the rough edges that bespoke his slave origins, some began to think that he must be a hoax and that perhaps the lack of specificity in his speeches about his own experiences in slavery indicated that he had never been a slave. Thus, by 1844, Douglass realized that his value to the abolitionist movement depended on making frank disclosures of his origins. The result was *Narrative of the Life of Frederick Douglass, an American Slave,* a slender volume of his slave recollections that revealed for the first time his original name, the names of his mother and grandmother, and the identity of his owners.

Such openness had its desired effect: Douglass's credibility as a bona fide victim of slavery was established. But that openness also made him highly vulnerable to a slave-catcher's effort to return him to Maryland. Consequently, his abolitionist allies decided that the time was ripe for him to make a speaking tour of antislavery societies in the British Isles.

Document drawn up to facilitate the purchase of Douglass's freedom by his British admirers

National Park Service, Frederick Douglass
National Historic Site, Washington, D.C.

During his stay in the British Isles, from August 1845 through early 1847, Douglass's appearances before antislavery meetings won him many admirers. Among the most ardent of his devotees was Ellen Richardson, who was determined that Douglass return to the United States relieved of the anxiety of being a fugitive slave who could be forced back into slavery at any time. She therefore began to raise funds to purchase Douglass's freedom from Thomas Auld. By late 1846 the money was in hand, and on November 30, Auld signed this document transferring ownership of Douglass to his brother Hugh, who twelve days later granted Douglass his freedom in exchange for $711.66.

Some American abolitionists regarded this transaction as an egregious betrayal of their movement's contention that no one had the "right to traffic in human beings." But it was easy to take that militant line when one's own freedom was not at stake. In any case, Douglass answered the objectors by reminding them that his freedom did not negate the authenticity of his slave's past, nor did it lessen his dedication as a crusader against slavery's evil.

Sojourner Truth   circa 1797–1883

Among the black abolitionists whom Douglass came to know before the Civil War, no one was more colorful than the former slave Sojourner Truth, who after 1850 combined her antislavery endeavors with advocacy of the country's newborn feminist movement. Tall, lanky, and simply dressed, she spoke in an unlearned but captivating dialect and stated her thoughts with a mystical religiosity that led Harriet Beecher Stowe to call her the "Libyan Sibyl." Of Truth, Douglass once wrote, "She cared very little for elegance of speech or refinement of manners. She seemed to please . . . best when she put her ideas in the oddest forms." With regard to Truth's indifference to refinement, Douglass knew all too well of what he spoke. When he first encountered her in 1844 at a utopian commune in Massachusetts, he had the distinct impression that she considered it "her duty to trip me up in my speeches and to ridicule my efforts to speak and act like a person of cultivation."

Randall Studio (active 1870s)
Albumen silver print, 14.4 × 10.3 cm
(5 $^{11}/_{16}$ × 4 $^{1}/_{16}$ in.), circa 1870
National Portrait Gallery, Smithsonian
Institution, Washington, D.C.

William Lloyd Garrison   1805–1879

During the three decades preceding the Civil War, no figure loomed more prominently in the crusade against slavery than William Lloyd Garrison, founding editor of the abolitionist newspaper the *Liberator*, and a pivotal force in both the New England and American antislavery societies. Garrison had a personal significance in Douglass's life. For it was the "holy fire" of Garrison's antislavery rhetoric that inspired Douglass's own activism in the abolitionist movement, and during his early years as a spokesman for the movement, Garrison served as his primary mentor.

By the early 1850s, however, the two men were bitterly estranged. Outwardly, the chief bone of contention was Douglass's open disagreement with Garrison's inflexible belief that because the Constitution recognized slavery's legal standing, the promotion of abolition through participation in the political structures set up under the Constitution was both futile and immoral. But friction on this point was perhaps only emblematic of a deeper cause for the alienation—Garrison's resentment that an ex-slave, whom he had helped to make into a noted public figure, should have the audacity to outgrow the need for his guidance and advice.

Nevertheless, Douglass never entirely lost his admiration for Garrison, and several years after their break, he described his onetime mentor as a "Moses, raised up by God, to deliver his modern Israel from bondage."

Unidentified artist
Oil on canvas, 76.2 × 63.5 cm (30 × 25 in.),
    circa 1855
National Portrait Gallery, Smithsonian
    Institution, Washington, D.C.; gift of Marlies
    R. and Sylvester G. March

An issue of William Lloyd Garrison's *Liberator*, November 25, 1842

Several months after his arrival in New Bedford, an agent for the abolitionist newspaper the *Liberator* came to Douglass's door asking him to subscribe. When Douglass explained that he was a recently escaped slave who could not yet spare the funds for this non-necessity, the agent put him on his subscription list anyway.

So began Douglass's education in the principles of the antislavery movement, and he relished every minute of it. Recalling his instantaneous passion for the *Liberator* when it began arriving at his home, he later observed, "I not only liked—I *loved* this paper."

Wendell Phillips   1811–1884

Martin Milmore (1844–1883)
Bronze, 71.1 cm (28 in.) height, 1869
National Portrait Gallery, Smithsonian
Institution, Washington, D.C.

In terms of his origins, Boston abolitionist Wendell Phillips could not have had less in common with the ex-slave Frederick Douglass. Educated at Harvard, this handsome and polished man was born into the heart of New England's old aristocracy, and wealth and social privilege had always been his as a matter of course. Yet Phillips was, perhaps more than any of the crusaders who shared the antislavery platform with Douglass, most sincerely in tune with the latter's egalitarian aims and outlook. Unlike many abolitionists, Phillips shared Douglass's conviction that while their main goal was elimination of slavery in the South, antislavery advocates were also obliged to fight for equal treatment of free blacks in the North. More important, he acted on that conviction, and in the twenty years before the Civil War, Phillips stood in the vanguard of those agitating for such issues as the desegregation of public schools in the North. Among the other signs of his dedication to racial equality was Phillips's rejection of the prevailing segregationist habits at inns and in public transportation. Once, while traveling with Douglass to an abolitionist meeting, he gave up his berth on a New York–bound boat after Douglass had been denied one, and instead spent a wakeful night keeping his companion company on deck.

Martin R. Delany   1812–1885

Douglass knew that southern slavery was not the only injustice against blacks in America and that, slave or free, African Americans of the pre–Civil War period lived daily with gross inequities that resulted from deeply rooted racial prejudices among whites, both North and South. Nevertheless, he never stopped believing "that there was no country . . . where the black man could more successfully elevate himself and his race than in the United States."

For his friend Martin Delany—who collaborated in the late 1840s in the founding of Douglass's abolitionist newspaper, the *North Star*—that was not the case. Thoroughly disillusioned with this country's capacity to mend its discriminatory ways, this physician and race reformer eventually concluded that the African American's salvation lay in establishing a separate black homeland outside of North America. By 1852 he had launched a campaign to sell this nationalism to others, and seven years later, he sailed for Africa to open the way for colonizing American blacks in the Niger Valley.

The Niger scheme never went beyond the planning stage, however, and during the Civil War Delany joined Douglass in working as a recruiter of black Union soldiers. Toward the war's end, he donned an army uniform himself and became the first African American to attain the rank of major.

Unidentified artist
Hand-colored lithograph, 55.2 × 43.8 cm
    (21 ³/4 × 17 ¹/4 in.), circa 1865
National Portrait Gallery, Smithsonian
    Institution, Washington, D.C.

Charles Remond   1810–1873

Among those traveling with Douglass on the abolitionist lecture circuit in the early 1840s was Charles Remond, a free-born black from Salem, Massachusetts. Eventually Douglass would eclipse Remond in fame and influence. Nevertheless, the well-spoken Remond could hold his own with the most eloquent of orators, and during his stay in London for the World Anti-Slavery Convention of 1840, he found himself lionized following his impromptu speech at Exeter Hall, in which he had characterized slavery as "a system of legalized murder." Douglass expressed his own high regard for Remond by naming one of his sons after him.

Samuel Broadbent (1810–1880)
Daguerreotype, 10.8 × 8 cm (4 1/4 × 3 1/8 in.), circa 1850
The Trustees of the Boston Public Library, Massachusetts

Henry Highland Garnet   1815–1882

James U. Stead (active circa 1877–?)
Albumen silver print, 11.6 × 9 cm
(4 9/16 × 3 9/16 in.), circa 1881
National Portrait Gallery, Smithsonian
Institution, Washington, D.C.

Having begun his abolitionist career as the protégé of William Lloyd Garrison, Douglass initially embraced the Garrisonian conviction that the only proper approach for fighting slavery was the peaceable appeal to moral conscience. When he attended his first National Convention of Colored Citizens in 1843, however, he encountered a man with quite a different tactical outlook: Henry Highland Garnet, a Presbyterian minister who had escaped slavery with his family in 1825. Described as "a perfect Apollo," the majestically handsome Garnet startled the convention by declaring it far better for the South's bondsmen to die in open insurrection than to "live slaves and entail . . . [their] wretchedness upon . . . [their] posterity."

Douglass abhorred this call to violence, and his speech challenging the wisdom of Garnet's sanguinary radicalism persuaded the convention to vote down an endorsement of Garnet's remarks. But by the 1850s, with slavery as implacably entrenched as ever, he drew closer to Garnet's views, and in 1857 he himself declared that "the slave's right to revolt is perfect, and only wants . . . favorable circumstances to become a duty."

Maria Weston Chapman   1806–1885

Unidentified photographer
Daguerreotype, 10.8 × 8.3 cm (4 ¼ × 3 ¼
   in.), circa 1846
The Trustees of the Boston Public Library,
   Massachusetts

As Douglass proved himself on the abolitionist circuit, he increasingly bristled at white abolitionists who patronizingly questioned his judgment and presumed to know better than he what was best for him. A case in point was the handsomely regal Maria Weston Chapman, a founding member of the Boston Female Anti-Slavery Society and a principal lieutenant to William Lloyd Garrison. When Douglass went to the British Isles in 1845 as a spokesman for the Garrisonian branch of American abolitionism, Chapman became apprehensive that he would ally himself with antislavery forces that were not in sympathy with Garrison's apolitical strategies. To guard against that, she asked an English associate to keep an eye on Douglass. Upon learning of this request, Douglass was outraged, and he soon informed her of his displeasure. "If you wish to drive me from the Anti-Slavery Society," he told her, "put me under overseership and the work is done." The allusion to an aspect of slavery in that retort was ironically apt, since Chapman's distrust of Douglass's judgment doubtless stemmed in large part from a perception that a black ex-slave, by definition, required close monitoring and guidance.

Elizabeth Cady Stanton (left), 1815–1902, and Susan B. Anthony, 1820–1906

Unidentified photographer
Gelatin silver print, 13.5 × 9.8 cm
(5 5/16 × 3 7/8 in.), circa 1870
National Portrait Gallery, Smithsonian
Institution, Washington, D.C.

With its concern for human rights, the antislavery movement provided a fertile ground for feminism. By the early 1850s, such abolitionist advocates as Elizabeth Cady Stanton and Susan B. Anthony were rapidly creating a movement calling for the liberation of women from a system of laws and customs that relegated them to a position inferior to men. Among Stanton and Anthony's most steadfast male allies in this new cause was Frederick Douglass. In fact, Douglass had been present at the birth of the American feminist movement in the summer of 1848 at a convention in Seneca Falls, New York. More important, he played a pivotal role there, when his support for Stanton's resolution calling for the enfranchisement of women persuaded the convention to adopt it, despite the misgivings of many delegates.

Douglass's speech, "The Claims of the Negro, Ethnologically Considered," 1854

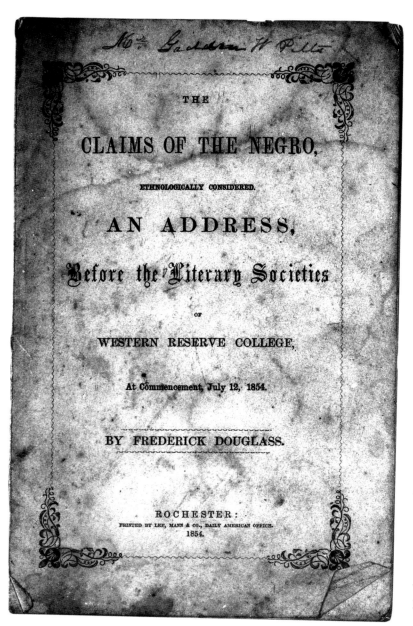

When the literary societies at Ohio's Western Reserve College asked Douglass to address them and their guests during the school's commencement week of 1854, the college's administrators were appalled. Apparently assuming that a self-educated ex-slave was by definition incapable of supplying a speech worthy of this academic occasion, they even pressured the students to withdraw their invitation. But the students stood firm. On the afternoon of July 12, 1854, Douglass was at Western Reserve, standing before a crowd of more than two thousand and demolishing point by point, in carefully measured and learned terms, the scientific evidence of the day alleging that blacks were inherently inferior to whites. Titled "The Claims of the Negro, Ethnologically Considered," the speech was an unalloyed triumph that in itself refuted notions of white superiority. Commenting on Douglass's success in meeting white academia on its own terms, the *New York Tribune* hailed it as the "turning of a new page."

THE NORTH STAR

RIGHT IS OF NO SEX—TRUTH IS OF NO COLOR—GOD IS THE FATHER OF US ALL, AND ALL WE ARE BRETHREN.

ROCHESTER, N. Y., FRIDAY, MARCH 10, 1848.

FREDERICK DOUGLASS, } EDITORS.
M. R. DELANY,

VOL. I. NO. XI.

CIRCULAR.

Rochester, January, 1853.

DEAR READER:—

You are interested in the welfare of all men—you desire to see slavery abolished—you want to see your country free—you believe in the power of truth, and in the efficiency of the press, as a means of getting the truth before the people. I feel, therefore, safe in asking you to lend me your assistance, in extending the circulation of my paper. Try and add one other name beside your own to my subscription list. I am in earnest. My paper has entered on its sixth volume. *It will continue to advocate, as it has ever done, the immediate and unconditional emancipation of every slave in this country and throughout the world.* To this end it will bring before its readers all the facts and arguments, which expose the legitimate abominations of slavery, and that serve to show the slave system to be a crime and a curse, incapable of excuse or palliation. It will aim to impress upon all Christian men the duty of remembering " them that are in the bonds as being bound with them," pointing out and exposing the pro-slavery action and position of political organizations. It will demand in the name of justice, liberty, and Christian fidelity, the total withdrawal of all church fellowship from slaveholders and their abettors. It will maintain the doctrines of the utter unconstitutionality of slavery, and show that the enactments in support of it, are no more to be respected as Laws, than are the adopted rules of pirates and other robbers, who band themselves together to plunder and to murder mankind.

It will make no compromise with slavery, or with pro-slavery parties, but will insist upon faithfulness to the slave at the ballot box, and will endeavor to concentrate the anti-slavery sentiment of the country, in that way and manner, at any given time, as shall, in the judgment of its editor, promise the greatest efficiency in the work of abolishing slavery. Devoted to the PRINCIPLES of the Liberty Party, it will hold them up for adoption by all who would act politically against slavery and kindred evils.

It will gladly be the medium through which GERRIT SMITH, the distinguished representative of the most radical type of political abolitionism, shall speak to the people. It will not be ashamed to regard him as a wise, as well as a faithful leader of the moral and political forces against slavery, or to make him its standard bearer. It will esteem the laws of God above the enactments of men ; and when the latter conflicts with the former, it shall go for adhering to the "higher law." It will hold the church and the clergy responsible for slavery ; and will appeal to them in the name of humanity, and according to the law of the living God, to break every yoke, and to let the oppressed go free. Those religious bodies which HAVE separated themselves, and which MAY separate themselves from the slave system, shall be encouraged and commended for their righteous position. All schemes of colonization, which look to the expatriation of the free colored people from their native land, the better to secure the slave in his chains, shall be sternly opposed. I shall contend for the immediate enfranchisement of colored citizens—for equal educational advantages—equal facilities for learning trades—equal rights in the use of public conveyances—equal justice before the law—equality in all the relations of life, making character and manhood, NOT color and features, the criterion of fitness for the enjoyment of rights and privileges. In a word, my columns shall be devoted to a defence of all the just rights of the human family, male and female, black and white, and without respect to country, nation or tongue. Aside from the intrinsic merits of the paper itself, it ought to be sustained because it has afforded, and does now afford, colored young men, who would find it impossible to learn the art of printing, an opportunity to accomplish that desirable object.

I ask you to give me your co-operation in my enterprize. Yours, truly,

FREDERICK DOUGLASS.

FREDERICK DOUGLASS' PAPER

IS PUBLISHED AT 25, BUFFALO STREET (OPPOSITE THE ARCADE.)

TERMS:

Single copy, one year	$2,00
Three copies, one year	5,00
Five copies, one year	8,00
Ten copies, one year	15,00
Single copy, six months	1,00
Ten copies, six months	8,00

Voluntary Agents are entitled to retain 50 cents commission on each new yearly subscriber, EXCEPT IN THE CASE OF CLUBS.

In making up clubs for FREDERICK DOUGLASS' PAPER, it is not requisite that the subscribers shall all be at one Post Office.

ADVERTISEMENTS, not exceeding ten lines, inserted three times for ONE DOLLAR ; every subsequent insertion, TWENTY-FIVE CENTS. Liberal reductions made on yearly advertisements.

All communications, whether on business, or for publication, should be addressed to FREDERICK DOUGLASS, ROCHESTER, NEW-YORK.

Frederick Douglass's weekly paper

The great admiration aroused by Douglass during his extended stay in the British Isles (1845–1847) not only led to a fundraising campaign for the purchase of his freedom; it also generated donations to finance a new business venture. Upon returning to the United States in the spring of 1847, Douglass brought with him sufficient capital to establish his own weekly abolitionist newspaper. His white antislavery mentors, among them William Lloyd Garrison and Maria Weston Chapman, tried to convince him that such an enterprise was unwise. But Douglass was not to be deterred; in December 1847, having established himself in Rochester, New York, he published the first issue of the *North Star*.

Renamed *Frederick Douglass' Paper* in 1851, the *North Star* was never a self-sustaining enterprise, and its finances continually teetered on the brink of disaster. Even so, it survived in one form or another for some fifteen years, and in that period it became a primary instrument for defining the demands, aspirations, and grievances of the country's African American community—free as well as slave.

Although abolition of slavery was the major focus of Douglass's newspaper, it was not the only one. As the last paragraph of this subscription circular indicates, Douglass was also determined not to miss any opportunity to promote the interests of free blacks in the North and demand for them the full complement of rights and privileges that they deserved.

The *North Star*, March 10, 1848 (*beneath*)
National Park Service, Frederick Douglass
    National Historic Site, Washington, D.C.

Circular promoting subscriptions to Douglass's newspaper, January 1853 (*atop*)
Clements Library, The University of
    Michigan, Ann Arbor

Douglass's *Oration, Delivered in Corinthian Hall, Rochester, July 5th, 1852*

ORATION,

DELIVERED IN CORINTHIAN HALL, ROCHESTER,

BY FREDERICK DOUGLASS,

JULY 5TH, 1852.

Published by Request.

ROCHESTER:
PRINTED BY LEE, MANN & CO., AMERICAN BUILDING.
1852.

In 1852 the Ladies' Anti-Slavery Society of Rochester, New York, invited Douglass to speak on the Fourth of July at Rochester's Corinthian Hall. He declined, not because he was previously engaged, but because he, as a black American, could not share the joyousness of that holiday. He did, however, agree to speak on the following day, and on July 5, he delivered the speech printed in the pamphlet here, more commonly known as "What to the Slave Is the Fourth of July?" In focusing on that question, Douglass fashioned an oration that was unforgivingly brutal in its attack on white America's failure to apply the ideals of the Declaration of Independence to its black slaves. Today, this speech is considered by many to be Douglass's finest, and some have called it the greatest abolitionist address ever delivered.

Department of Special Collections, Syracuse University Library, New York

These dolls were made by Cynthia Hill
of New Bedford, Massachusetts, where
Douglass had first settled after his escape
from slavery. Fashioned in the late 1850s,
they were meant to celebrate Douglass's
transformation from tattered slave to dig-
nified free man of consequence. More
generally, the dolls served as a reminder
that it was not the slave's race that kept
him down but the degradations imposed
upon him by his white masters.

Frederick Douglass doll and slave doll

New Bedford Whaling Museum,
    Massachusetts

John Brown   1800–1859

Undoubtedly the most radical abolitionist whom Douglass ever consorted with was the fiery-eyed John Brown. Believing firmly that the sins of slavery justified resorting to violence, Brown first put this conviction into practice in the mid-1850s, when he organized a small armed band of guerrillas to wage war against slaveholding settlers in the newly organized Kansas Territory. But Brown's ambitions extended far beyond that limited action. By early 1858, he had made Douglass privy to his scheme for leading an army of antislavery warriors into the hills of western Virginia and setting up a guerrilla enclave, whose mission would be to precipitate a slave uprising that could eventually sweep the entire South.

Brown tried to recruit Douglass into the scheme. Although Douglass was intrigued and at times supportive, he ultimately backed away from direct involvement. That did not, however, save him from being implicated in the conspiracy when it came to an end with a disastrous raid on Harpers Ferry, Virginia, and Brown's capture by federal troops in October 1859. With a warrant out for his arrest, Douglass sought refuge in England and did not return home until several months after Brown had been tried and hanged. By then Brown had been transformed into a martyr to freedom, and in the summer of 1860, Douglass told an abolitionist group that he counted knowing Brown "among the highest privileges" of his life.

Ole Peter Hansen Balling (1823–1906)
Oil on canvas, 76.2 × 63.5 cm (30 × 25 in.),
    circa 1859
National Portrait Gallery, Smithsonian
    Institution, Washington, D.C.

Gerrit Smith   1797–1874

Following his break with William Lloyd Garrison, one of Douglass's closest allies in the abolitionist movement was Gerrit Smith, a princely landowner from Madison County, New York, who devoted much of his life to philanthropy and various reforms. Among other things, Smith became Douglass's fiscal angel, and time and again he came to the rescue when Douglass's newspaper stood on the verge of bankruptcy. Smith also played a part in introducing Douglass to the possibilities of resorting to political activism in promoting the antislavery cause. A founder of the abolitionist Liberty Party, Smith was that organization's presidential candidate in the election of 1848. Four years later, he won election to the House of Representatives, where he soon joined in the unsuccessful struggle to block passage of the Kansas-Nebraska bill, a measure that opened new western territories to settlement by slaveholders.

Daniel Huntington (1816–1906)
Oil on canvas, 105.4 × 90.2 cm (41 1/2 × 35 1/2
    in.), 1874
Madison County Historical Society, Oneida,
    New York

"Practical Illustration of the Fugitive Slave Law"

This cartoon—showing Secretary of State Daniel Webster being ridden by a rapacious southern slave-catcher who has come to snatch a black woman from the North—was a commentary on the Fugitive Slave Law of 1850. Passed as a salve to the South, the law substantially increased federal law-enforcement cooperation in the capture of fugitive slaves and required a slaveholder to supply only minimal proof of ownership before having an alleged runaway returned to him.

Implementation of this statute outraged Douglass, along with all other abolitionists. More important, it further radicalized him. Once he had believed that peaceful agitation was the only proper vehicle for fighting slavery. But now, with the federal government standing squarely in the southern corner on the runaway issue, he was convinced that far stronger measures were justified. If it took life-threatening armed violence to prevent enforcement of the "monstrous and inhuman" Fugitive Slave Law, that was quite agreeable to him. "Every slave-hunter," he declared, "who meets a bloody death in his infernal business, is an argument in favor of the manhood of our race."

Unidentified artist
Lithograph, 28.4 × 36.4 cm (11 3/16 × 14 5/16 in.), circa 1850
Prints and Photographs Division, Library of Congress, Washington, D.C.

The Resurrection of Henry Box Brown
at Philadelphia

Unidentified artist
Lithograph, 27 × 40 cm
(10 5/8 × 15 3/4 in.), 1850
Prints and Photographs Division,
Library of Congress,
Washington, D.C.

One of the cleverest escapes from slavery in pre–Civil War America was that of Henry "Box" Brown, who in the late 1840s spirited himself to freedom hunched up in a cargo box that was sent via commercial shipper from Virginia to Philadelphia. The success of this ploy was widely publicized by abolitionists, and it eventually inspired this cartoon, showing the fugitive Brown emerging from his cargo box while Frederick Douglass assists in removing the box's lid.

Douglass was not present at Brown's arrival in Philadelphia, but he was included in the scene simply because of his prominence as an abolitionist and fellow runaway slave. Present or not, he was heartily irritated that particulars about Brown's flight from slavery had been made public. Writing in 1855, he lamented, "Had not Henry Box Brown and his friends attracted slaveholding attention to the manner of his escape, we might have had a thousand *Box Browns* per annum."

The abolitionist movement conducted its war against slavery largely with moralizing rhetoric, but it also backed up its words with action. By the 1840s, many antislavery northerners were serving as links in a relay network that guided runaway slaves to remote safe havens in the North and Canada, where they could live without fear of recapture. Known as the Underground Railroad, the clandestine operation had one of its centers in Rochester, which was an important jumping-off spot for slaves seeking asylum in Canada. Thus when Douglass settled in Rochester in late 1847, he inevitably became involved, and finding shelter for escaped slaves until it was safe to send them on the last leg of their trip to Canada quickly became a part of his daily routine. In this note, Douglass asks Miss Porter of the Rochester Ladies' Anti-Slavery Society to supply funds for getting a runaway to his Canadian destination. In local abolitionist parlance, this was known as arranging to "ship a bale of Southern goods."

Douglass's note requesting financial aid for runaway slaves, October 18, 1857

Miss Porter:

William Oborne — came to us last night from Slavery. He looks fully able to take care of himself, but being destitute, he needs for the present, a little assistance to get him to Canada — $2,50 will be quite sufficient.

Your Truly.

Frederick Douglass —

Rochester. Oct 13. 1857

Clements Library, The University of Michigan, Ann Arbor

No war but an Abolition war; no peace but an Abolition peace; liberty for all, Chains for none; the black man a soldier in war, a laborer in peace; a voter at the South as well as at the North; America his permanent home, and all Americans his fellow-countrymen. Such, fellow-citizens, is my idea for the mission of the war.

Frederick Douglass,
"Mission of the War,"
February 13, 1864

THE CIVIL WAR

In late 1860, the escalating rancor over slavery between North and South came to a head with the election of Abraham Lincoln to the presidency on the moderately antislavery Republican ticket. In the wake of that event, eleven southern states eventually seceded to form their own confederacy, and by late April 1861, the North was girding itself for a war to coerce the South back into the Union.

Many who watched the onset of the Civil War were horrified. But Douglass unashamedly welcomed a resort to arms, and in May 1861 he declared, "God be praised! that it has come at last." For although the North's only stated objective in the early stages of the conflict was preservation of the Union, Douglass knew that a northern triumph almost assuredly meant an end to slavery as well. He was also aware that he had a role to play in shaping that triumph. His wartime activities included pressuring Lincoln to make slave emancipation part of the North's war aims and serving as a recruiter of black enlistments for the Union army. But perhaps most important, even before emancipation became a reality, Douglass stood in the vanguard of those urging national policies to ensure that the country's freed slaves would enjoy a full measure of the privileges to which their new status would entitle them.

Douglass and other abolitionists are attacked in Boston on the eve of the Civil War by a mob accusing them of causing disunion. Engraving from *Harper's Weekly,* December 15, 1860

Abraham Lincoln with Figure of Liberty Unshackled

In his several encounters with Abraham Lincoln during the Civil War, Douglass found him to be a warm, shrewd, and personable man. Moreover, when Douglass spoke at the dedication of the larger-than-life version of this statue in Washington, D.C., in 1876, his words indicated that he shared the deep popular veneration that had transformed Lincoln since his assassination from mere mortal into the unassailably saintly Great Emancipator.

But Douglass's regard for Lincoln had not always been so high. At one point during the Civil War, he had even snarled that the motto of the nation's sixteenth President was: "Do evil by choice, right from necessity."

Among the factors that inspired these damning words was Douglass's impatience with the political pragmatism that so often overshadowed moral considerations in Lincoln's decisions on major wartime issues. The most noteworthy case in point was slave emancipation: While from the war's outset, Douglass urged the adoption of federal policies that unequivocally identified the Union cause with the eradication of slavery, Lincoln himself balked at such a course until he was sure that the climate of popular opinion was ripe for it.

Thomas Ball (1819–1911)
Bronze, 82.3 cm (32 in.) height, circa 1870
Houghton Library, Harvard University,
    Cambridge, Massachusetts

Printed version of Lincoln's Emancipation Proclamation, January 1, 1863

Despite vocal prodding from abolitionists, including Douglass, Lincoln steadfastly refused to make the abolition of slavery a northern goal in the early stages of the Civil War, lest doing so would alienate slaveholding border states that remained loyal to the Union. By mid-1862, however, Lincoln's concern for enhancing the moral weight of the Union cause in the eyes of the world convinced him that it was time to act. In September 1862, he announced the Emancipation Proclamation, which would take effect on January 1, 1863, and declared all slaves free in those regions of the South still loyal to the Confederacy.

In terms of freeing any slaves, the proclamation had no immediate impact. Nevertheless, it guaranteed that a northern triumph in the war would bring about slavery's ultimate demise. And that was quite enough for Douglass. Declaring January 1, 1863, "a day for poetry and song," he focused on the Emancipation Proclamation's spirit, which had "a life and power" that went well "beyond its letter."

William Roberts (1829?–?)
Wood engraving, 50.1 × 38.1 cm (19 $^{11}/_{16}$ × 15 in.), 1864
National Portrait Gallery, Smithsonian Institution, Washington, D.C.

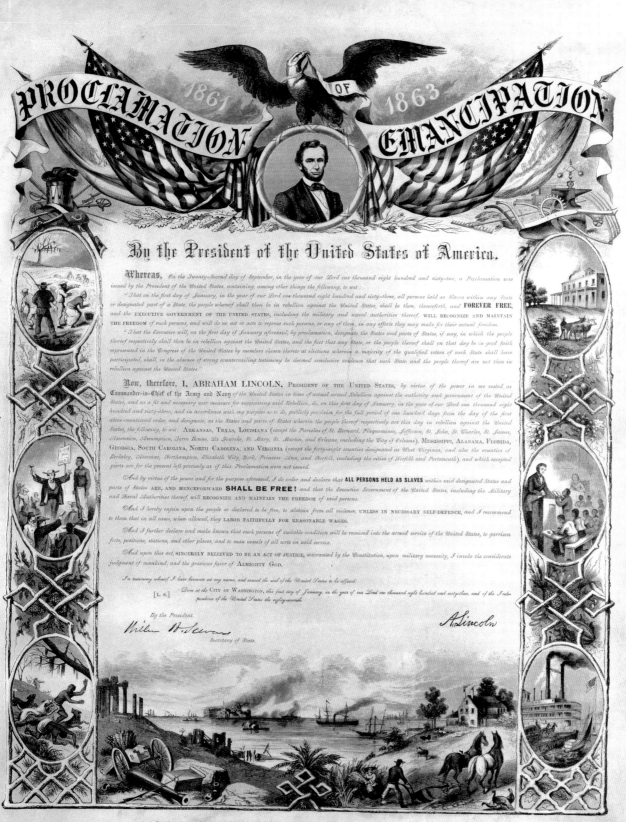

MEN OF COLOR, TO ARMS!

A Call by Frederick Douglass.

When first the Rebel cannon shattered the walls of Sumter, and drove away its starving garrison, I predicted that the war then and there inaugurated would not be fought out entirely by white men. Every month's experience during these two dreary years has confirmed that opinion. A war undertaken and brazenly carried on for the perpetual enslavement of colored men, calls logically and loudly upon colored men to help to suppress it. Only a moderate share of sagacity was needed to see that the arm of the slave was the best defence against the arm of the slaveholder. Hence with every reverse to the National arms, with every exulting shout of victory raised by the slaveholding Rebels, I have implored the imperilled nation to unchain against her foes her powerful black hand. Slowly and reluctantly that appeal is beginning to be heeded. Stop not now to complain that it was not heeded sooner. It may, or it may not have been best—that it should not. This is not the time to discuss that question. Leave it to the future. When the war is over, the country is saved, peace is established, and the black man's rights are secured, as they will be, history with an impartial hand, will dispose of that and sundry other questions. Action! action! not criticism, is the plain duty of this hour. Words are now useful only as they stimulate to blows. The office of speech now is only to point out when, where and how to strike to the best advantage. There is no time for delay. The tide is at flood that leads on to fortune. From east to west, from north to south the sky is written all over with "now or never." Liberty won by white men would lack half its lustre. Who would be free themselves must strike the blow. Better even to die free than to live slaves. This is the sentiment of every brave colored man among us. There are weak and cowardly men in all nations. We have them among us. They will tell you that this is the "whiteman's war;" that you will be "better off after than before the war;" that the getting of you into the army is to "sacrifice you on the first opportunity." Believe them not—cowards themselves, they do not wish to have their cowardice shamed by your brave example. Leave them to their timidity, or to whatever other motive may hold them back.

I have not thought lightly of the words I am now addressing to you. The counsel I give comes of close observation of the great struggle now in progress—and of the deep conviction that this is your hour and mine.

In good earnest, then, and after the best deliberation, I, now, for the first time during the war, feel at liberty to call and counsel you to arms. By every consideration which binds you to your enslaved fellow countrymen, and the peace and welfare of your country; by every aspiration which you cherish for the freedom and equality of yourselves and your children; by all the ties of blood and identity which make us one with the brave black men now fighting our battles in Louisiana, in South Carolina, I urge you to fly to arms, and smite with death the power that would bury the Government and your liberty in the same hopeless grave. I wish I could tell you that the State of New York calls you to this high honor. For the moment her constituted authorities are silent on the subject. They will speak by and by, and doubtless on the right side; but we are not compelled to wait for her. We can get at the throat of treason and Slavery through the State of Massachusetts.

She was first in the war of Independence; first to break the chains of her slaves; first to make the black man equal before the law; first to admit colored children to her common schools, and she was the first to answer with her blood the alarm cry of the nation—when its capital was menaced by rebels. You know her patriotic Governor, and you know Charles Sumner—I need add no more.

Massachusetts now welcomes you to arms as her soldiers. She has but a small colored population from which to recruit. She has full leave of the General Government to send one regiment to the war, and she has undertaken to do it. Go quickly and help fill up this first colored regiment from the North. I am authorized to assure you that you will receive the same wages, the same rations, the same equipments, the same protection, the same treatment and the same bounty secured to white soldiers. You will be led by able and skillful officers—men who will take especial pride in your efficiency and success. They will be quick to accord to you all the honor you shall merit by your valor—and see that your rights and feelings are respected by other soldiers. I have assured myself on these points—and can speak with authority. More than twenty years unswerving devotion to our common cause, may give me some humble claim to be trusted at this momentous crisis.

I will not argue. To do so implies hesitation and doubt, and you do not hesitate. You do not doubt. The day dawns—the morning star is bright upon the horizon! The iron gate of our prison stands half open. One gallant rush from the North will fling it wide open, while four millions of our brothers and sisters shall march out into Liberty! The chance is now given you to end in a day the bondage of centuries, and to rise in one bound from social degradation to the plane of common equality with all other varieties of men. Remember Denmark Vesey of Charleston. Remember Nathaniel Turner of South Hampton; remember Shields, Green, and Copeland, who followed noble John Brown, and fell as glorious martyrs for the cause of the slaves. Remember that in a contest with oppression, the Almighty has no attribute which can take sides with oppressors. The case is before you. This is our golden opportunity—let us accept it—and forever wipe out the dark reproaches unsparingly hurled against us by our enemies. Win for ourselves the gratitude of our country—and the best blessings of our prosperity through all time. The nucleus of this first regiment is now in camp at Readville, a short distance from Boston. I will undertake to forward to Boston all persons adjudged fit to be mustered into this regiment, who shall apply to me at any time within the next two weeks.

FREDERICK DOUGLASS.

Rochester, March 2, 1863.

"Men of Color, to Arms! A Call by Frederick Douglass," 1863

Douglass had urged the enlistment of blacks in the Union army practically from the Civil War's outset. But it was not until the summer of 1862 that Congress finally lifted a legal ban on blacks in the military, and only after the Emancipation Proclamation did Lincoln's administration give its blessing to efforts to raise black recruits in great numbers. Shortly thereafter, Douglass agreed to travel the North as a recruiting agent for the all-black Fifty-fourth Massachusetts Regiment. One of his first acts in that capacity was to pen the message for this broadside, urging able-bodied black men of the North to join in the crusade to deliver their southern brethren from bondage.

The C. Fiske Harris Collection on the Civil War and Slavery of the Providence Public Library, Rhode Island

Douglass's two sons, Lewis (*left*) and Charles, in Union army uniforms

Two of Douglass's first recruits into the Union army were his sons Lewis and Charles, both of whom served in the African American Fifty-fourth Regiment from Massachusetts. Lewis became the Fifty-fourth's first sergeant major and was a participant in the regiment's most noted battlefield encounter with Confederate forces—the Union's ill-fated assault on Fort Wagner in South Carolina on July 18, 1863.

Frederick Douglass Papers, Moorland-Spingarn Research Center, Howard University, Washington, D.C.

Newly enlisted black soldiers at Camp William Penn near Philadelphia

P. S. Duval and Son Lithography
Company (active 1857–1879)
Chromolithograph, 52.1 × 35.6 cm
(20 ¹/₂ × 14 in.), 1863
Library Company of Philadelphia,
Pennsylvania

When Douglass became a recruiter of black soldiers for the Union cause early in 1863, he had no illusions that black enlistees would be safe from racial abuse and discrimination in an overwhelmingly white army. "Colored men going into the army and navy," he warned, "must expect annoyance. They will be severely criticized and even insulted." Nevertheless, since the Emancipation Proclamation had made slavery's abolition a northern war aim, he believed that blacks had to serve simply as a matter of racial self-respect. As he put it, "Liberty won by white men would lack half its lustre."

MEN OF COLOR!
TO ARMS! TO ARMS!
NOW OR NEVER

This is our Golden Moment. The Government of the United States calls for every Able-Bodied Colored Man to enter the Army

For Three Years' Service

And join in Fighting the Battles of Liberty and Union.

A MASS MEETING

Of Colored Men, will be held

ON MONDAY, JULY 13,

AT 8 O'CLOCK, AT

CHESTER, DELAWARE CO., PA.

To promote Recruiting Colored Troops for Three Years or the War.

FREDERICK DOUGLASS

And other Distinguished Speakers, will Address the Meeting.

U. S. Steam-power Job Printing Establishment, S. W. Corner of Third and Chestnut Streets, Philada.

Poster for an army recruitment meeting where Douglass was to speak, 1863

Some of Douglass's army-recruiting efforts in northern black communities met with disappointing results, and a Philadelphia gathering where he tried to persuade young black males to don a soldier's uniform netted only one enlistment. The reasons behind that outcome were easy to understand: Black soldiers were paid less than white soldiers, their equipment was often inferior, and by and large they could not expect to become commissioned officers. Worse yet, if they were captured in battle, the Confederacy's laws and policies exposed them to the hazards of being summarily shot or sold into slavery.

When Douglass initially went recruiting, he urged prospective black soldiers to overlook these negative factors, because what they would be fighting for was of such transcendent importance to their people. But Douglass eventually concluded that he could not in good conscience continue to encourage men to risk their lives in the face of such conditions. By early August 1863, he had resigned as a recruiter, and although he later agreed, at Lincoln's urging, to help organize black troops along the Mississippi River, he never actually took that position.

Library Company of Philadelphia,
Pennsylvania

The storming of Fort Wagner, July 18, 1863

The Union assault on Fort Wagner in South Carolina was an utter disaster, with northern dead and wounded exceeding 1,500, while Confederate casualties stood at 174. But as far as Douglass was concerned, it was a triumph in one very important respect: The group leading the Union charge had been members of the black Fifty-fourth Regiment from Massachusetts. Although the situation had been hopeless from the outset, these soldiers had fought honorably and bravely. In short, the black soldier had proved his mettle under the worst of conditions and demonstrated to a leery white northern public that valor was not something that only whites were capable of.

Currier and Ives Lithography Company
    (active 1857–1907)
Lithograph, 22.9 × 31.8 cm (9 × 12 ¹/₂ in.),
    image, 1863
Library Company of Philadelphia,
    Pennsylvania

Letter endorsed by Lincoln to facilitate Douglass's projected trip to help organize black troops in Mississippi, August 10, 1863

Department of the Interior.
Washington D.C. Augt. 10. 1863

To whom it may concern,

The bearer of this, Frederick Douglass, is known to us as a loyal, free, man, and is, hence, entitled to travel, unmolested,—

We trust he will be recognized everywhere, as a free man, and a gentleman.

Respectfully,

J.P. Usher
Secy.

S.C. Pomeroy
U.S.S.
Kansas

Pass the Bearer Fredruk Douglass who is known to me to be free man
M. Blair Png

Concur. Abraham Lincoln
Aug. 10. 1863.

In late July 1863, after indicating that he was going to stop recruiting black soldiers because of his dissatisfaction with racial discrimination in the army, Douglass was assured, in an interview with Abraham Lincoln, that most of his grievances would in time be addressed. That was enough to persuade him to honor the request to serve as an assistant to General Lorenzo Thomas in raising and organizing black troops near Vicksburg, Mississippi. Douglass, however, had accepted on the understanding that he would receive an officer's commission, and when the commission failed to materialize, he decided against taking the assignment.

First page of Douglass's letter to Lincoln outlining a scheme to subvert southern slavery, August 29, 1864

In an interview at the White House on August 19, 1864, Douglass discussed with Lincoln how a network of black federal agents could sap the Confederacy's war-making capacities by infiltrating the South and conducting a campaign to encourage its slave labor force to escape to the safety of Union lines. Ten days later, Douglass followed up with this letter outlining some of his specific ideas on how such a conspiracy might be made to work. The plot, however, never went beyond the discussion stage.

Manuscript Division, Library of Congress, Washington, D.C.

It is true that we are no longer slaves, but it is equally true that we are not yet quite free. We have been turned out of the house of bondage, but we have not yet been fully admitted to the glorious temple of American liberty. We are still in a transition state and the future is shrouded in doubt and danger.

Frederick Douglass,
"We Are Not Yet Quite Free,"
August 3, 1869

THE ERA OF RECONSTRUCTION

As the Civil War drew to a close in the spring of 1865, Douglass was in his late forties, and he felt that "the noblest and best" part of his life was over. The feeling was understandable. With slavery now gone, so too was the cause that had energized him and been his main focus for the past twenty-five years.

But Douglass was not long in finding a new sense of purpose. Although the Civil War had ended slavery, the Union victory by no means guaranteed that the newly freed people of the South would be substantially better off than they had been as slaves. In fact, as southern states raced to enact "black codes" imposing sharp restraints on the liberties of their black populations, it seemed possible that slavery was about to be restored to the former Confederacy in all but name. Thus, Douglass was soon devoting much of his time to pressuring for federal policies that would safeguard—by force if necessary—the rights of blacks and promote their chances for a truly free and productive life.

In the post–Civil War decade known as the Reconstruction era, many of the actions that Douglass championed were taken, and he could take pride in knowing that his earlier advocacy of such measures as the enfranchisement of black males had given impetus to their realization. But the satisfaction Douglass felt was bittersweet at best. In the face of an unrelenting racism that by the late 1870s was undoing the advances that blacks had made during Reconstruction, he unhappily realized that the need for his services as a defender of his people's interests would almost certainly never go away.

The labor of a former slave, convicted of a crime, is sold off after the Civil War. Engraving from *Leslie's Illustrated Weekly Newspaper,* January 19, 1867

Replica of a bust of Frederick Douglass modeled in the 1870s

In July 1872 Douglass moved from Rochester, New York, where he had lived for twenty-five years, to Washington, D.C. The following fall, a group of Rochester's citizens—wanting to mark the fact that Douglass had spent some of the most fruitful years of his public life in their midst—commissioned the local sculptor Johnson Mundy to fashion his likeness in marble. By late 1873 Mundy had completed the portrait, and six years later it was presented to the city and placed on view at the University of Rochester. This plaster likeness was made from Mundy's original marble version and belonged to Douglass himself.

C. Hess (lifedates unknown), after Johnson Mundy
Plaster, 91.4 cm (36 in.) height, circa 1875
National Park Service, Frederick Douglass National Historic Site, Washington, D.C.

Frederick Douglass in his late forties

Samuel Root (1819–1889)
Carte-de-visite, 29.8 × 24.1 cm
  (11 3/4 × 9 1/2 in.) framed, circa 1865
Ronald L. Harris

Andrew Johnson's Reconstruction and How It Works

Following Lincoln's assassination in 1865, his vice president, Andrew Johnson, succeeded to the presidency, and it initially fell to him to determine federal policies regarding punishment of the South for making war on the Union and help its former slave population adjust to freedom. Essentially, Johnson chose a course that promised no retribution against the South's white establishment and left the region's blacks defenseless against local attempts to sharply constrict their political, social, and economic rights in the postwar era. Many northerners viewed this policy as a betrayal of the Union cause, and in this cartoon Johnson is cast as a malevolent Iago, who, while professing friendship for the nation's blacks, permits their welfare to fall victim to unrestrained southern racism.

Not surprisingly, Douglass agreed with this characterization, and in February 1866 he was part of a black delegation that went to the White House to persuade Johnson to protect the freedmen of the South. Johnson, however, was barely courteous and remained unmoved. Soon Douglass was joining others in a campaign that ended in Congress's replacement of Johnson's southern policies with measures decidedly more sympathetic to black interests.

Thomas Nast (1840–1902)
Wood engraving for *Harper's Weekly*, 34.6 × 21.7 cm (13 5/8 × 8 9/16 in.), published September 1, 1866
National Portrait Gallery, Smithsonian Institution, Washington, D.C.

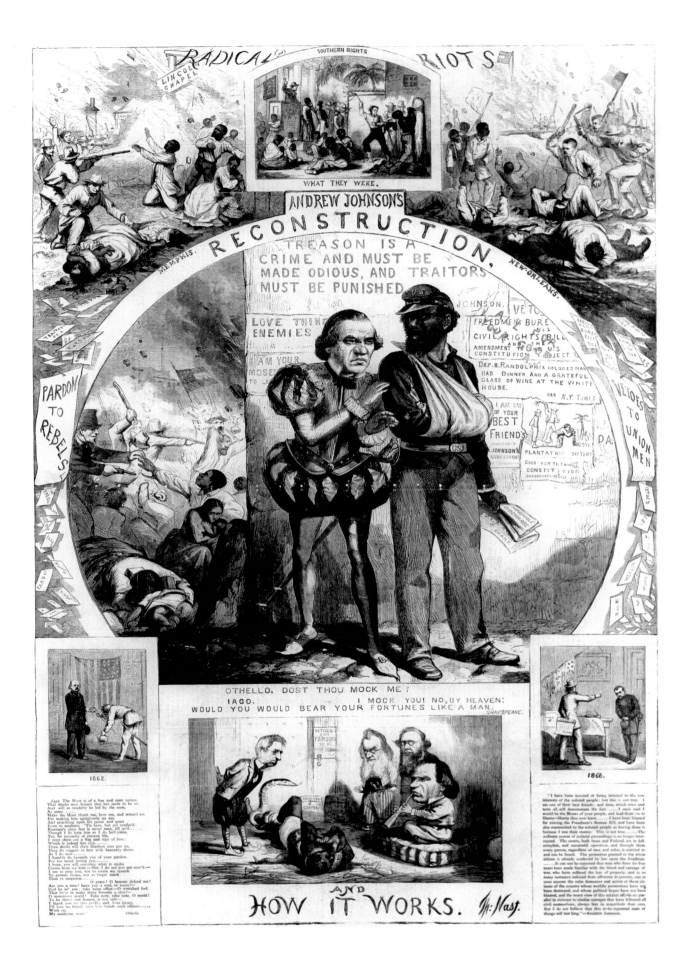

Entered according to act of Congress in the year 1872 by Currier & Ives in the Office of the Librarian of Congress at Washington.

ROBERT C. DE LARGE, M.C. of S.Carolina.   JEFFERSON H. LONG, M.C. of Georgia.

U.S. Senator H.R.REVELS, of Mississippi.   BENJ.S.TURNER, M.C. of Alabama.   JOSIAH T. WALLS, M.C. of Florida.   JOSEPH H. RAINY, M.C. of S.Carolina.   R. BROWN ELLIOT, M.C. of S.Carolina.

THE FIRST COLORED SENATOR AND REPRESENTATIVES.

In the 41st and 42nd Congress of the United States.

NEWYORK, PUBLISHED BY CURRIER & IVES, 125 NASSAU STREET.

74

The First Colored Senator and Representatives

Among the most significant fruits of Congress's Reconstruction policies was the political empowerment of southern blacks, which by the early 1870s had led to the election of African Americans to Congress for the first time. Pictured here are the first blacks to serve in that body: *(left to right)* Senator Hiram R. Revels and Representatives Benjamin S. Turner, Robert C. De Large, Josiah Walls, Jefferson F. Long, Joseph H. Rainey, and Elliot R. Brown.

In the face of this landmark change in Congress's makeup, many of Douglass's intimates—including one of his sons—urged him to move to an area of the South with a large black electorate and seek a Senate or House seat for himself. Had he done so, his prestige as a chief spokesman for his people would doubtless have made him a shoo-in. But Douglass had "small faith in . . . [his] aptitude as a politician" and rejected the idea, feeling that he could serve black interests better as a lecturer and publicist.

Currier and Ives Lithography Company
   (active 1857–1907)
Lithograph, 22 × 32 cm (8 5/8 × 12 1/2 in.),
   1872
National Portrait Gallery, Smithsonian
   Institution, Washington, D.C.

The Result of the Fifteenth Amendment

For Douglass, the most significant event of the Reconstruction era was the passage in 1870 of the Fifteenth Amendment to the Constitution, which prohibited denying the vote to anyone on the basis of race. Reflecting the euphoric view of this print celebrating the amendment's enactment, Douglass considered it the mainspring from which all other advances for blacks would come. For, with a place in the political process assured, he reasoned, blacks could now wield real influence and, in the process, shape their own destinies at last.

Unfortunately, voting was not the panacea for blacks that Douglass expected it would be. Moreover, in the years following its passage, the Fifteenth Amendment became increasingly meaningless, as the federal government lost interest in enforcing it, and as the South devised ways to disenfranchise blacks that supposedly did not violate the amendment.

Metcalf & Clark, publishers (active 1870s)
Hand-colored lithograph, 48 × 62.6 cm
(18 7/8 × 24 5/8 in.), 1870
Prints and Photographs Division, Library of
Congress, Washington, D.C.

Charles Sumner   1811–1874

Douglass once claimed that no one had done more to advance the interests of African Americans than Charles Sumner and that, as far as blacks were concerned, nothing could ever "dim in any wise the brightness" of Sumner's reputation. Such effusiveness was understandable. During his tenure as a senator from Massachusetts from 1851 until his death in 1874, Sumner often exhibited a lack of political tact and had put off many—even his allies—with his abrasive, lofty manner. Nevertheless, his unswerving opposition to slavery before the Civil War and his abiding interest in promoting the welfare of African Americans after the war were undeniable. In fact, it could be said that his rhetoric of moral urgency became a defining force in Congress's attempt, during the Reconstruction decade, to protect the rights of the country's newly freed blacks against white racism.

Edgar Parker (1840–1892)
Oil on canvas, 137.1 × 86.4 cm (54 × 34 in.), 1874
National Portrait Gallery, Smithsonian Institution, Washington, D.C.

Frederick Douglass in 1883

This portrait of Douglass shows him holding the baton that symbolized his authority during his tenure as marshal of the District of Columbia. The painter of the likeness was Sarah J. Eddy, who came from a comfortably fixed, reform-minded family of Rhode Island and Massachusetts, and whose parents had come to know Douglass through the abolitionist movement. Douglass sat for this portrait during two visits to Rhode Island in the spring and summer of 1883.

Sarah J. Eddy (1851–1945)
Oil on canvas, approximately 127 × 86.4 cm
(50 × 34 in.), 1883
National Park Service, Frederick Douglass
National Historic Site, Washington, D.C.

The American people have this lesson to learn: That where justice is denied, where poverty is enforced, where ignorance prevails, and where any one class is made to feel that society is an organized conspiracy to oppress, rob, and degrade them, neither persons nor property will be safe.

Frederick Douglass,
"Southern Barbarism,"
April 1886

LATER YEARS

By the mid-1870s, Douglass was clearly the elder statesman of the country's African American community. He was also one of its chief links with the Republican Party, which he never stopped regarding as the party most inclined to defend his people's interests. With the close of the Reconstruction era in 1877, there was progressively less basis for that faith, as the GOP turned from its concern for black freedmen to a preoccupation with economic issues related to industrial expansion. Nevertheless, Douglass remained ever faithful to the party of Lincoln, and in return for his campaign efforts on behalf of Republican presidential candidates, he was rewarded with a number of appointed offices. After serving as marshal of the District of Columbia during Rutherford B. Hayes's administration, he was appointed by President James Garfield as the District's recorder of deeds, and in 1889 President Benjamin Harrison selected him to be the United States minister to Haiti.

While these offices made Douglass's later years comfortable and secure, they did not lull him into complacency. As American blacks—especially in the South—saw the rights and opportunities that were supposedly secured for them during Reconstruction disappearing under a tidal wave of racial hatred and institutionalized discrimination, Douglass remained as compelling as ever when speaking out against the injustices to his people.

When asked shortly before his death what course black youth should follow in the face of continuing racism in this country, he answered, "Agitate! Agitate! Agitate!" Behind that thundering imperative lay an unwavering conviction, born of more than fifty years of protest, that unjust conditions, no matter how hopelessly well-entrenched, must never be accepted passively.

District of Columbia marshal Frederick Douglass at President James Garfield's inauguration.
Engraving from *Life and Times of Frederick Douglass* (1881)

Douglass with delegates for a mission to Santo Domingo, 1871

In 1871 President Ulysses S. Grant appointed Douglass secretary to a diplomatic mission charged with investigating the desirability of annexing the Caribbean nation of Santo Domingo as a United States territory. By identifying Douglass with this venture, Grant hoped to counter critics who claimed that American annexation was detrimental to the interests of Santo Domingo's black majority. But despite the mission's report in favor of annexation, Congress refused to give the matter any consideration.

In this picture, taken in Key West, Florida, after the mission's return from Santo Domingo, Douglass stands *(center right)* with the mission's members: *(left to right)* Andrew White, Benjamin Wade, and Samuel Gridley Howe.

Unidentified photographer
Albumen silver print, 18 × 26.2 cm
    (7 × 10 $^5/_{16}$ in.), 1871
Anacostia Museum, Smithsonian Institution,
    Washington, D.C.

**Douglass receiving congratulations
for his appointment as marshal
of the District of Columbia in 1877**

The advent of Republican Rutherford B. Hayes's presidential administration marked the end of federal involvement in the postwar reconstruction of the South, along with the abandonment of southern blacks to the mercies of the racism of their white neighbors. It also brought Douglass's appointment as United States marshal of the District of Columbia. The two events were not unrelated. On the one hand, the federal pullout in the South was meant to palliate the whites of that region. On the other, for those

troubled by the dismal implications of the pullout for blacks, Douglass's selection as marshal was intended to signify Hayes's commitment to advancing the interests of African Americans.

When Douglass's appointment became known, many lawyers practicing in the federal courts of Washington were stunned and incensed that a black man was to be administering an office directly involved with their daily work. Despite the protest, the Senate endorsed Douglass, who served as marshal until 1881.

Unidentified artist
Wood engraving, published in *Frank Leslie's Illustrated,* April 7, 1877
Prints and Photographs Division,
Library of Congress, Washington, D.C.

Bandanna from the Republican presidential campaign of 1888

PROTECTION TO HOME INDUSTRIES

GEN. BEN. HARRISON

Ralph E. Becker Collection, National Museum of American History, Smithsonian Institution, Washington, D.C.

By the late 1880s, southern blacks were rapidly losing the right to vote, through a combination of intimidation and legal chicanery. Huge numbers had also been reduced to an unbreakable cycle of impoverishment under the region's sharecropping system, and mob lynchings of blacks suspected of wrongdoing were a growing fact of life in the South. As a result, Douglass went to the Republican national convention of 1888 intent on convincing the party that it must renew its historic role as defender of black interests. To some extent he found a sympathetic audience, and written into the Republican platform was a promise to bring federal authority to bear in ensuring the nation's blacks of their right to vote.

Immensely heartened by this turn of events, Douglass became an active campaigner for the GOP's presidential candidate, Benjamin Harrison. By election day, he had stumped six states on Harrison's behalf. Unfortunately, once Harrison was in office, neither he nor his allies in Congress could deliver on their platform promise to blacks. Although a measure to guarantee the franchise to southern blacks passed through the House, it eventually died in a Senate filibuster.

Douglass's appointment as United States minister to Haiti, June 26, 1889

As reward for his campaign help in putting Benjamin Harrison in the White House, Douglass was appointed minister to the Republic of Haiti. While serving in that post, he became involved in negotiations to lease a coaling station from Haiti, which Harrison's administration dearly wanted as a means of establishing an American presence in the Caribbean. Douglass had no difficulty in supporting that objective, and he proved more than willing to assist Rear Admiral Bancroft Gherardi, who was in charge of the negotiations with the Haitian government.

When the Haitians ultimately refused to agree to a lease, however, Douglass was roundly attacked in the press and accused of undermining the talks. But if anyone was to be blamed, it should have been Gherardi, whose imperious approach to the discussions inevitably offended the Haitian president and his foreign minister.

National Park Service, Frederick Douglass National Historic Site, Washington, D.C.

Douglass in Haiti with three unidentified women

Unidentified photographer
Albumen silver print, 10.5 × 8.9 cm
   (4 ¹/₈ × 3 ¹/₂ in.), circa 1890
Frederick Douglass Papers, Moorland-
   Spingarn Research Center, Howard
   University, Washington, D.C.

"Lessons of the Hour"

Lessons · of · the · Hour
·BY·
Hon. Frederick Douglass,

Metropolitan A. M. E. Church,
WASHINGTON, D. C.

BALTIMORE:
PRESS OF THOMAS & EVANS.
1894.

Manuscript Division, Library of Congress,
Washington, D.C.

Douglass's last major speech in defense of his people was "Lessons of the Hour." Delivered in varying forms on a number of occasions in 1892 and 1893, the oration focused on the disturbing increase in the South of mob lynchings and burnings of black men who had been accused of raping white women. That rape was a heinous act, Douglass readily admitted. But it could not justify, he declared, executing a man charged with that crime without a trial. Besides, as Douglass skillfully demonstrated, rape charges were being leveled against blacks in many cases merely to provide a pretext for mob violence. In short, lynching, he asserted, was just the latest—and most barbaric—tool in the South's longstanding conspiracy to keep blacks in a subservient position through intimidation.

"Lessons of the Hour" drew many accolades, and a senator even recommended it to his fellow legislators on the Senate floor. But as historian William McFeely pointed out recently, "It did absolutely no good." Lynching continued to be a hazard of life for blacks, especially in the South, for many decades to come.

Anna Murray Douglass   1813?–1882

Douglass's first wife, Anna, was the daughter of manumitted slaves, and by the time the two met in the late 1830s, she was earning her living as a domestic servant in Baltimore. Married to Douglass shortly after his escape from slavery in 1838, she remained illiterate throughout her life and was disinclined to share in any way in her husband's public career. So it is not surprising that the couple's relationship seems to have become more distant as Douglass grew intellectually and his experiences broadened.

Julius Ulke Studio (active 1870s)
Albumen silver print, 14.7 × 9.6 cm
 (5 3/4 × 3 3/4 in.), circa 1875
Frederick Douglass Papers, Moorland-
 Spingarn Research Center, Howard
 University, Washington, D.C.

Helen Pitts Douglass   1838–1903

Johnson Brothers (active 1880s)
Albumen silver print, 16.5 × 10.7 cm
(6 ½ × 4 ¼ in.), 1880–1890
National Park Service, Frederick Douglass
National Historic Site, Washington, D.C.

In January 1884, about a year and a half after the death of his first wife, Douglass married Helen Pitts, a white woman educated at Mount Holyoke Seminary who worked for him at the District of Columbia's Recorder of Deeds office. The stir caused by this event was considerable, and the couple soon found themselves an object of controversy among blacks and whites alike. Members of the immediate family of both the bride and groom expressed displeasure, and some wondered how Douglass's illustrious reputation as a black leader would fare now that he had violated nineteenth-century America's deeply felt taboo against mixed marriages. In the view of a black government worker, it would not fare very well at all. Labeling the marriage "a disgraceful thing," he solemnly predicted that "this will crush Mr. Douglass as far as his influence with the colored people is concerned."

The marriage, however, was a happy one, and although some never could quite accept it, it did not seem to diminish Douglass's prestige in the long run.

Rosetta Douglass, 1839–1904
J. H. Kent (lifedates unknown)
Albumen silver print, 9.5 × 5.7 cm
   (3 3/4 × 2 1/4 in.), not dated
National Park Service, Frederick
   Douglass National Historic Site,
   Washington, D.C.

Lewis H. Douglass, 1840–1908
Hartman and Taylor (active 1860s)
Albumen silver print, 10.2 × 6.4 cm
   (4 × 2 1/2 in.), circa 1860
National Park Service, Frederick
   Douglass National Historic Site,
   Washington, D.C.

Frederick Douglass, Jr., 1842–1892
Samuel M. Fassett (active 1855–1875)
Albumen silver print, 10.7 × 6.5 cm
   (4 × 2 1/2 in.), not dated
National Park Service, Frederick
   Douglass National Historic Site,
   Washington, D.C.

Charles Remond Douglass, 1844–1920
Rice Photography (active 1880s)
Albumen silver print, 10.1 × 6.3 cm
(4 × 3 in.), circa 1885
National Park Service, Frederick
Douglass National Historic Site,
Washington, D.C.

Douglass's children
Rosetta Douglass Sprague
Lewis H. Douglass
Frederick Douglass, Jr.
Charles Remond Douglass

Being the offspring of a great man can give children an edge in making their ways in life. But in the case of Douglass's children, that edge never proved of much value, and none of them ever realized anything more than moderate success. Charles Douglass earned his living for the most part as a clerk in several federal bureaus, brothers Frederick and Lewis became printers, and sister Rosetta married a man who proved unsteady at best in his ability to provide for his family.

In part, the modesty of these achievements may have been related to the drives and abilities of Douglass's children. But it was also true that racial discrimination in nineteenth-century America inhibited advancement even for blacks who were well connected. A case in point was Lewis Douglass, who was barred from joining a printers' union because of his color and then vilified for being a scab when he took a job for wages below union scale. Lewis's father likened this treatment to cutting off a man's ears and then claiming that this maiming now gave one "the right to pluck out his eyes."

Douglass working at his desk at his home,
Cedar Hill, in Washington, D.C.

Unidentified photographer
Albumen silver print, 19.7 × 24.8 cm
(7 ³/₄ × 9 ³/₄ in.), circa 1890
National Park Service, Frederick Douglass
National Historic Site, Washington, D.C.

Ida B. Wells-Barnett   1862–1931

In his last years, Douglass came to know Ida B. Wells, a southern black woman who by the early 1890s was emerging as one of the African American community's most forceful agitators for racial justice and who collaborated with Douglass on several ventures. Chief among their joint enterprises was the pamphlet *Why the Colored American Is Not in the World's Columbian Exposition,* which sought to publicize, to both domestic and foreign visitors to the 1893 exposition, the oppressive inequalities suffered daily by blacks in democratic America. Wells wrote the main text, Douglass provided the introduction, and together they orchestrated the pamphlet's distribution from the Haitian Pavilion, where Douglass was serving as official host.

Last photograph ever taken of Douglass

The frailties of old age slowed Douglass down in his last years, but he remained an imposing presence to the end. He also never lost his power to hold audiences spellbound with his fiery eloquence. In 1893, for example, on a hot summer day in Festival Hall at the World's Columbian Exposition in Chicago, he refused to be ruffled by jeers and catcalls from white racists among his listeners and, throwing his prepared speech aside, held forth extemporaneously for an hour on the racial sins of the United States. All in all, this unplanned oration proved to be a "masterpiece of wit, humor, and actual statement of conditions" that met with thunderous applause.

Notman Photographic Company (active 1878–1927)
Albumen silver print, 22.2 × 18.7 cm (8 3/4 × 7 3/8 in.), circa 1895
Sophia Smith Collection, Smith College, Northampton, Massachusetts

Earthenware pitcher commemorating
Douglass's life, produced shortly after his death

Patented by J. E. Bruce (lifedates unknown)

Red earthenware, 26.2 × 26.2 cm (10 ⁵/₁₆ × 10 ⁵/₁₆ in.),
    1896

National Museum of American History, Smithsonian
Institution, Washington, D.C.

Small version of the Frederick Douglass memorial erected in Rochester, New York, four years after his death

Sidney W. Edwards (lifedates unknown)
Bronze, 79 cm (31 in.) height, circa 1898
National Park Service, Frederick Douglass
    National Historic Site, Washington, D.C.

Undoubtedly the community that took greatest pride in its association with Douglass was Rochester, New York, where he had resided for twenty-five of the most eventful years of his life. On the morning of February 21, 1895—the day following Douglass's death—some Rochester citizens were already talking of raising a public statue to his memory. In June 1899 that talk finally became a reality when, amid much fanfare and speech-making, the larger-than-life version of the statue reproduced here was unveiled in the city's Highland Park.

Set on its pedestal facing north to symbolize Douglass's pre–Civil War quest for his own freedom, the monument was meant to portray Douglass as he had appeared before an audience at about the time of the enactment of the Fifteenth Amendment in 1870. Euphoric over this event, which supposedly guaranteed the vote to blacks, he expressed his joy in personal terms, declaring, "I appear before you to-night for the first time in the more elevated position of an American citizen."

Portrait of Frederick Douglass
done shortly after his death

Based on a photograph, this pastel likeness of Douglass was the work of Daniel Freeman, an artist and photographer who for many years was a leader in Washington, D.C.'s African American art community.

Daniel Freeman (1868–after 1919)
Pastel on paper, 67.3 × 54.6 cm
   (26 1/2 × 21 1/2 in.), 1895
Jerome C. Gray

NOTES ON SOURCES

BEGINNINGS IN SLAVERY

"I have nothing cruel or shocking," in Frederick Douglass, *My Bondage and My Freedom* (New York, 1969), p. 129. "Incapable of a noble action," quoted in Dickson Preston, *Young Frederick Douglass* (Baltimore, 1980), pp. 107–8. "Sold south" and "living death," in Douglass, *The Life and Times of Frederick Douglass* (New York, 1962), p. 174. "Rascality of slaveholders," in Douglass, *My Bondage and My Freedom,* p. 165.

SPOKESMAN FOR ABOLITION

"With the utmost difficulty," in Douglass, *My Bondage and My Freedom,* p. 358. "He is a swarthy Ajax," quoted in Benjamin Quarles, *Frederick Douglass* (New York, 1968), p. 105. "A *little* of the plantation," in Douglass, *My Bondage and My Freedom,* p. 362. "Fine specimen of an orator," quoted in Philip S. Foner, *Frederick Douglass: A Biography* (New York, 1964), p. 55. "Right to traffic in human beings," quoted in Foner, *Frederick Douglass,* p. 73. "She cared little," quoted in Charles Sheffield, ed., *The History of Florence, Massachusetts* (Florence, Mass., 1895), p. 132. "Moses, raised up by God," in Douglass, *My Bondage and My Freedom,* pp. 354–55. "I not only liked," in Douglass, *My Bondage and My Freedom,* p. 354. "That there was no country," in Douglass, *The Frederick Douglass Papers,* Series One: *Speeches, Debates, and Interviews,* ed. John W. Blassingame and John R. McKivigan (New Haven, Conn., 1979–1992), vol. 2, p. 476. "A system of legalized murder," quoted in Miriam L. Usrey, "Charles Lenox Remond, Garrison's Ebony Echo, World Anti-Slavery Convention, 1840," *Essex Institute Historical Collections* 106 (April 1970): 124. "A perfect Apollo," quoted in Leon Litwack and August Meier, eds., *Black Leaders of the Nineteenth Century* (Urbana, Ill., 1988), p. 137. "The slave's right to revolt," quoted in Waldo E. Martin, *The Mind of Frederick Douglass* (Chapel Hill, N.C., 1984), p. 167. "If you wish to drive me," quoted in Foner, *Life and Writings of Frederick Douglass* (New York, 1950), vol. 1, p. 144. "Turning of a new page," quoted in Audrey McCluskey and John McCluskey, "Frederick Douglass on Ethnology: A Commencement Address at Western Reserve College, 1854," *Negro History Bulletin* 40, no. 5 (September–October 1977): 748. "Among the highest privileges," quoted in Foner, *Frederick Douglass,* p. 182. "Monstrous and inhuman," quoted in Foner, *Frederick Douglass,* p. 133. "Had not Henry Box Brown," in Douglass, *My Bondage and My Freedom,* p. 323. "Ship a bale of Southern goods," quoted in Foner, *Frederick Douglass,* p. 130.

DOUGLASS AND THE CIVIL WAR

"God be praised!" quoted in David W. Blight, *Frederick Douglass' Civil War: Keeping Faith in Jubilee* (Baton Rouge, La., 1989), p. 59. "Do evil by choice," quoted in ibid., p. 182. "A day for poetry and song," quoted in Foner, *Frederick Douglass*, p. 209. "Colored men going into the army," quoted in Foner, *Frederick Douglass*, p. 213.

DOUGLASS AND THE ERA OF RECONSTRUCTION

"The noblest and best," in Douglass, *Life and Times*, p. 373. "Small faith," ibid., p. 398. "Dim in any wise," in Douglass, *Frederick Douglass Papers*, ed. Blassingame and McKivigan, vol 4., p. 269.

DOUGLASS'S LATER YEARS

"Agitate! Agitate! Agitate!," quoted in Foner, *Frederick Douglass*, p. 371. "It did absolutely no good," in William S. McFeely, *Frederick Douglass* (New York, 1991), p. 381. "A disgraceful thing," in *Washington Star*, January 25, 1884. "The right to pluck out his eyes," quoted in Foner, *Frederick Douglass*, p. 219. "Masterpiece of wit, humor," quoted in Ida B. Wells-Barnett, *Crusade for Justice: The Autobiography of Ida B. Wells*, ed. Alfreda M. Duster (Chicago, 1970), p. 119. "I appear before you to-night," quoted in John W. Thompson, *An Authentic History of the Douglass Monument* (Freeport, N. Y., 1971), p. 156.

FOR FURTHER READING

Blight, David W. *Frederick Douglass'
Civil War: Keeping Faith in Jubilee.*
Baton Rouge, La.: University of
Louisiana Press, 1989.

Douglass, Frederick. *The Frederick
Douglass Papers,* Series One:
Speeches, Debates, and Interviews.
Ed. John W. Blassingame and John
R. McKivigan. 5 volumes. New
Haven, Conn.: Yale University
Press, 1979–1992.

———. *Life and Times of Frederick
Douglass.* 1892. New York: Collier
Books, 1962.

———. *My Bondage and My Freedom.*
1855. Introduction by Philip S.
Foner. New York: Dover Publica-
tions, 1969.

———. *Narrative of the Life of Frederick Douglass, an American Slave.* 1845.
Ed. David W. Blight. Boston: Bedford Books of St. Martin's Press,
1993.

Foner, Philip S. *Frederick Douglass:
A Biography.* New York: Citadel
Press, 1964.

———. *Life and Writings of Frederick
Douglass.* 4 volumes. New York:
International Publishers, 1950.

Huggins, Nathan I. *Slave and Citizen:
The Life of Frederick Douglass.* Boston: Little, Brown, 1980.

Litwack, Leon, and August Meier, eds.
*Black Leaders of the Nineteenth Cen-
tury.* Urbana: University of Illinois
Press, 1988.

McFeely, William S. *Frederick Douglass.*
New York: W. W. Norton, 1991.

McPherson, James M. *The Negro's Civil
War.* New York: Random House,
1965.

Martin, Waldo E. *The Mind of Frederick Douglass.* Chapel Hill: University
of North Carolina Press, 1984.

Preston, Dickson J. *Young Frederick
Douglass.* Baltimore: Johns Hopkins
University Press, 1980.

Quarles, Benjamin. *Black Abolitionists.*
New York: Oxford University Press,
1969.

———. *The Negro and the Civil War.*
Boston: Little, Brown, 1953.

This book was acquired for Smithsonian Institution Press by Mark Hirsch. The manuscript was edited by Frances Stevenson, Dru Dowdy, and Katherine Gibney at the National Portrait Gallery and by Jack Kirshbaum of Smithsonian Institution Press. The production of the book was managed by Ken Sabol. The book was designed by Linda McKnight. The text was composed on an Agfa Selectset 5000 by Graphic Composition, Inc., of Athens, Georgia. The text typeface is Adobe Caslon, originally designed by William Caslon in 1725 and redesigned for Adobe Systems, Inc., by Carol Twombly. Caslon was a typeface commonly in use during the nineteenth century. The display type is Adobe Bodoni Poster Compressed. The book was printed on 80-lb Lustro Offset Enamel paper by D. W. Friesen and Sons of Altona, Manitoba, Canada.

Frederick Douglass Memorial Spoon

Silver, 15.3 cm (6 in.), after 1895
Jerome C. Gray